Portugal's African Wars

Portugal's African Wars

**Angola
Guinea Bissao
Mozambique**

**ARSLAN HUMBARACI
and
NICOLE MUCHNIK**

THE THIRD PRESS
Joseph Okpaku Publishing Company, Inc.
444 Central Park West, New York, N. Y. 10025

Library of Congress Catalogue Card Number: 72-93676

ISBN: 0-89388-072-8

First printing

Printed in Great Britain

Dedication

This book is dedicated to Dr Kenneth Kaunda and Mwalimu Julius Nyerere without whose support the liberation struggle in Southern Africa would not have been where it is today.

I have had the rare privilege of serving both and addressing them as 'Brother' or 'Comrade' President. Some, out of ignorance or malice, may misinterpret the latter term which with men like Kenneth Kaunda and Julius Nyerere takes its full human value. I wish there were more leaders like them, in the West and in the East, for it would be a better world. I am only sorry that in the last two years some elements in Kaunda's Zambian administration, who have conducted a 'dialogue' with South Africa under the table and done their utmost to stab the MPLA in the back, should have isolated Kaunda and misled Zambia into an unholy alliance with General Mobutu of Zaïre.

My friend and co-author Nicole Muchnik joins me in this dedication.

A.H.

Acknowledgements

Thanks are due to Susan Watson for her assistance in writing Parts I and III, for reading Part II and proof-reading the entire book, and to Dr Agostinho Neto for permission to reprint the poem which appears on p. 233.

Contents

Author's Note

DURING the final stages of production of this book General Spinola, Portugal's new President, has made overtures to freedom fighters in Africa. Will these overtures result in freedom? I am no futurologist and all I can formulate is an advanced, if personal, opinion.

I believe the new General-President, in spite of his recent metamorphosis into a 'liberal', remains profoundly conservative in outlook and will do his utmost to bring about a NATO-approved neo-colonial solution, particularly as regards Angola. In Guinea Bissao, poverty-stricken and strategically unimportant, the new masters of Portugal can afford to be more generous and recognise total independence – with the exception, I believe, of the Cape Verde Islands. In Mozambique, my guess is that Spinola will have to concede part of the country to FRELIMO, while turning a blind eye to a South African-backed UDI in the southern part of the country. Finally, in Angola, the fabulously rich, unexplored Eldorado of Africa, whose wealth is necessary not only to Portugal but to the USA themselves, the struggle for the future will provide a key test both for the new Lisbon regime and for the MPLA. Right across the Portuguese political spectrum one man is named as the only *interlocuteur valable*. He is Dr Agostinho Neto, the MPLA leader. The test of his undeniably great statesmanship is approaching. Will he survive and be able to lead Angola to a real independence through all the obstacles and temptations which the whole 'right', white, black and international, is strewing in his path?

May 1974   A.H.

PART I
by ARSLAN HUMBARACI

Foreword

A F R I C A is in ferment – its huge Southern expanse and a tiny area along its North-West coast in the grip of revolution. Events succeed each other at a quick pace and happen with great suddenness – like bushfires. Publishers – and writers – can find themselves lagging behind.

What was considered a far fetched allegation at the time the first draft of this book was ready at the beginning of 1972 – i.e. the inevitable increasing involvement of South African and Rhodesian forces in Mozambique and Angola – has now become an accepted fact to informed opinion in the West. Similarly, it is now also agreed that FRELIMO is within the defence perimeters of the giant Cabora Bassa hydroelectric scheme, having already successfully attacked the key Portuguese base of Sitim, eighteen kms from the site of the dam and probing towards the port of Beira from the north of the Punge river.

In the chapter 'The Border of Human Decency', the plots – to liquidate leaders of Liberation Movements as well as Presidents Kaunda and Nyerere – must be updated in the face of fresh murderous evidence: an attempt to kill Dr Agostinho Neto, the Angolan leader and the *doyen* of the revolt in Portuguese colonies and, simultaneously, disrupt the MPLA's advance from the East. This plot bore the same stamp as the assassination of Neto's brother-in-arms, Amilcar Cabral.

Further concrete evidence of General Mobutu's collusion with imperialism was obtained as this book was going to press and, regretfully, a detailed map could not be included to show where 'a second Kuwait' has been found off the Cabinda enclave and how oil struck off Zaïre is to be routed through Portuguese-occupied territory to the terminals of the Gulf Oil Co.

No doubt the near future is to bring many other such revelations and surprises – for Western opinion long lulled into apathy, the now-embattled white minority regimes and for the liberation forces themselves caught in the dialectic of revolution. But this is the picture, so far, of Southern Africa's 'Vietnam'.

Geneva/Africa/London, December 1971–October 1973

Angola: Some Basic Facts

Area: 1,246,700 kms.², including the Cabinda enclave (7,270 kms.²).

Population: 4,840,719 inhabitants (including 13,499 in Cabinda) of which '172,529 *branco*, 53,392 *mestiço*, 4,604,362 *preto* and 166 others' according to the 1960 census as published in Portugal's *Anuário Estatistico, Vol. II, Ultramar 1967.* Official estimates for 1970 put the population at 5,700,000, of which some 400,000 are white.

Capital: Luanda – town, 224,540 inhabitants; district, of same name, 33,789 kms.² and 346,763 inhabitants.

Principal exports: coffee, cotton, fishmeal, maize, timber, iron ore, oil, diamonds.

Balance of payments with foreign countries:

	1967	1968	1969	million escudos
Merchandise	+ 1,204	+ 622	+ 188	,,
Current invisibles & capital	+ 334	+ 646	+ 1,367	,,
TOTAL	+ 1,358	+ 1,268	+ 1,555	,,

National Liberation Movement and date of its foundation: Movimento Popular de Libertaçao de Angola (MPLA); December 10, 1956, in Luanda.

Leadership of MPLA: Dr Agostinho Neto, President.

Outbreak of revolution: February 4, 1961.

ANGOLA

Railways ►►► Main Roads ═══

0 ____ 150m MPLA Advance ➤ Provinces LUNDA

Liberated areas by December 1973: approximately 1/3 of the country (see map on page 16).

Budget (1973) of Portuguese occupational forces in Angola:

Army	1,595,556,000	escudos
Air Force	311,000,000	,,
Navy	130,680,000	,,
TOTAL	2,037,236,000	,,

Number of Portuguese troops in Angola: 60 to 80,000 according to various sources quoted by the UN (Doc. A/8423/Add.4 of 28/9/1971) – Portuguese and African para-military forces known as *Forças Militarizadas* are not included in these figures.

Guerilla armed forces: 7,000 according to the Portuguese MPLA will not disclose any figures on this subject.

São Tomé and Príncipe

Area: These two islands, situated in the Biafra Gulf, West of Gabon, total a land surface of 964 kms.² São Tomé is 854 kms.² and Príncipe, 120 kms. to the north, is 110 kms.

Population: 73,811 according to the provisional figures of the 1970 census, of which approximately 60% are *autócton*, the remainder, including some 3,000 Europeans, being from Angola, Cape Verde and Mozambique. São Tomé has 69,149 inhabitants.

Guinea Bissao and the Cape Verde Archipelago: Some Basic Facts

(This information applies to the whole former colony of Guinea Bissao of which (see below) two thirds became the independent republic of Guinea Bissao on September 1973.)

Area: 36,125 kms.², including the Bijagós Archipelago. The Cape Verde Archipelago, which lies some 600 kms. off the African coast, consists of ten islands and five islets and is divided into two groups – the Barlavento (Windward) and the Sotavento (Leeward); it consists of 4,033 kms.² of land.

Population: 530,000 inhabitants according to the 1969 UN Demographic Yearbook. Latest census details, dating from 1950, reported 4,586 *mestiços*, 2,263 Europeans, 1,478 assimilated Africans and 11 Indians. No information is available on the 1971 population census in this country.

The Cape Verde population was of 252,000 inhabitants in 1970 and according to 1950 census results the ethnic composition of the Archipelago was *mestiço* 69·0%, African 28·84% and European 2·06%. Lisbon predicts a population explosion – 440,000 by 1990 and 600,000 by the year 2000.

Capital: Bissao. Estimated population 26,000.

Praia, in the island of Santiago, of the Sotavento Group, for the Cape Verde Archipelago. Praia had 45,079 inhabitants in 1960, and it measures 469·4 kms.²

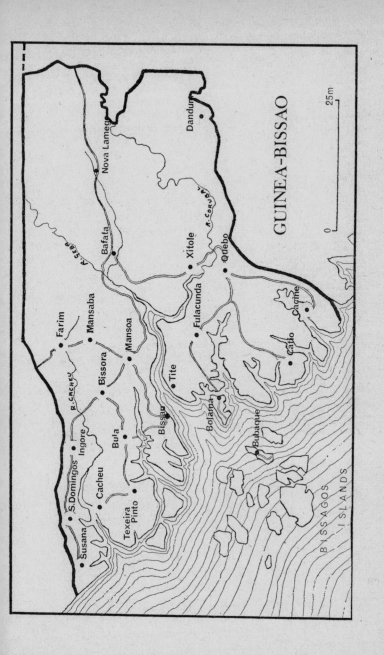

GUINEA-BISSAO

Principal exports: None of significance.

Balance of Payments with foreign countries: No recent statistics exist for Guinea Bissao where the trade deficit was of 494·9 million escudos, in 1968.

In Cape Verde, the balance of payments was as follows:

	1968	1969	million escudos
Merchandise	−169·8	−248·8	,,
Current invisibles	+209·2	+224·9	,,
Capital Movements	− 7·4	− 8·3	,,
TOTAL	+ 32·0	− 32·2	,,

National Liberation Movement and date of its foundation: Partido Africano da Independência da Guiné e Cabo Verde (PAIGC); September 1956, in Bissao.

Leadership of PAIGC: Amilcar Cabral, Secretary General until his death on 20 January 1973; replaced by Aristide Pereira on 20 July 1973.

Outbreak of revolution: 3 April 1961.

Liberated areas by December 1973: Approximately two-thirds of continental Guinea Bissao (see map on page 19). Guinea Bissao proclaimed itself a republic on 24 September 1973 and appointed Luiz Cabral President of the Council of State.

Budget of Portuguese occupation forces in Guinea Bissao:

Army	48,000,000	escudos
Air Force	58,598,000	,,
Navy	90,000,000	,,
TOTAL	196,768,000	,,

In the Archipelago of Cape Verde, the 1971 estimate indicates an increase of 44% in allocation for the PSP, the *Polícia de Segurança Pública*, and of 31% for the DGS, the *Direcçao General de Segurença*, the former PIDE:

	1969	1970	1971	million escudos
National Defence	4·7	5·1	3·5	,,
PSP	3·1	3·2	4·6	,,
DGS	1·4	1·4	2·3	,,
TOTAL	9·2	9·7	10·4	,,

Number of Portuguese troops in Guinea Bissao: 30 to 35,000 excluding Portuguese-led African troops and other components of *Forças Militarizadas.*

No figures available for Cape Verde where three major military posts were established in 1970 against possible PAIGC landings.

Guerilla armed forces: 5,000 in Guinea Bissao according to the Portuguese. A compilation of Portuguese General Staff communiqués would however indicate that between 1963 and 1966, PAIGC suffered '10,927' losses. PAIGC, like MPLA and FRELIMO will not disclose any figures on its strength.

Mozambique: Some Basic Facts

Area: 771,125 kms.[2]

Population: 6,578,604 inhabitants, of which 6,430,530
Africans, 97,268 Europeans, 31,465 '*mistos*' and 19,341
Asians according to the 1960 census. Official figures published in 1969, in *Boletim Trimestral* (No. 77/78) of the
Banco Nacional Ultramarino put the population at
7,169,400 in 1967. An unofficial estimate of the Standard
Bank Review, of Johannesburg, put the population at
8,000,000 in 1970, of which 7,750,000 Africans, 210,000
whites and persons of mixed descent and 40,000 Asians.

Capital: Lourenço Marques – town, 178,565 inhabitants;
district of the same name, 436,916 inhabitants.

Principal exports: Cotton, cashew nuts, sugar, tea, copra.

Balance of Payments with foreign countries:

	1967	1968	1969	million escudos
Merchandise ...	−1,618	−1,484	−2,540	,,
Current invisibles & capital	+2,541	+2,556	+2,586	,,
TOTAL	+ 923	+1,072	+ 46	,,

National Liberation Movement and date of its foundation:
Frente de Libertaçao de Mocambique (FRELIMO);
June 1962, in Dar es Salaam.

Leadership of FRELIMO: Eduardo Mondlane, President

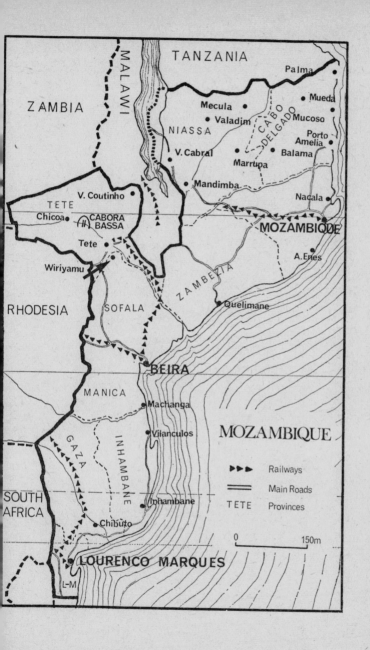

(assassinated on 3 February 1969). The actual leaders are: Samora Machel (President), and Marcelino Dos Santos (Vice-President), both members of the Presidency Council.

Outbreak of revolution: 25 September 1964.

Liberated areas by December 1973: approximately 20% of the country (see map on page 23).

Budget (1971) of Portuguese occupation forces in Mozambique:

Army	....	822,239,133	escudos
Air Force	......	230,000,000	,,
Navy	....	86,000,000	,,
TOTAL	......	1,145,293,133	,, —or $45,000,000.

Number of Portuguese troops in Mozambique: 60,000 in 1969, according to the UN (Doc. A/8023/Add.3 of 5/10/1970) – Portuguese and African para-military forces known as *Forças Militarizadas* are not included in these figures.

Guerilla armed forces: 3 to 4,000 according to Portuguese sources. FRELIMO will not disclose any figures on this subject.

The Rule of Law
Universal Declaration of
Human Rights

PREAMBLE – Whereas it is essential, if man is not to be
compelled to have recourse, as a last resort, to rebellion
against tyranny and oppression, that human rights should
be protected by the rule of law

Introduction

Milestones on the Great North Road

THE real power behind the war Portugal has now been waging for the last ten years in her colonies, Angola, Guinea Bissao and Mozambique, is not Portugal herself.

Portugal is too small and poor a country to be able to perform, by herself, an effort which is proportionately eight times bigger than the American war effort in Vietnam. Without NATO's direct and indirect assistance, the war in the last colonies in the African continent, would have already ended.

But NATO too is only one part of the picture of Southern Africa, where the dominating power is South Africa – backed by financial interests of the Western bloc.*

When President Nixon meets President Pompidou in the Azores – we shall see later on why this location was chosen – to discuss the West's monetary situation, what the press does not even mention is the fact that the world's monetary situation is based on the straightforward exploitation of the African miners in South Africa, which produces over 75 per cent of the total output of gold in the non-communist world. Forced labourers used in South African mines include those sent from Mozambique and Angola, by contract, between Pretoria and Lisbon.*

Similarly, what the public at large ignores, but NATO

certainly does not, is that the *status quo* in Southern Africa in general, and in Portugal's African colonies in particular, is already being maintained by South Africa – economically, politically and in the last resort, militarily. South African forces – army, air force and navy – are already operative in Angola and Mozambique and, of course, Rhodesia.*

The government of South Africa is based on minority rule* and its official policy is the racialist one of *apartheid* and the rigid application of the stringent laws needed to enforce it. According to the London *Sunday Times*, 'Of all the executions judicially performed in the world every year, half occur in just one country – South Africa'. We could add to this, the fact that every year, over 3,000 Africans are prosecuted for statutory offences under the various 'Pass Laws', influx control and related laws. During the year ending 30 June 1970, 496,000 Africans with sentences and 257,651 unsentenced, were committed to prison; the daily average in prison in South Africa was 90,555. The prison population included 4,700 breast-fed infants, and 187 babies were born to (African) mothers in prison; 340 persons 'died' in prison and 84 were 'officially' hanged. Reverting to the *Sunday Times*: 'South Africa has the world's largest judicial building – the Johannesburg Central Magistrates' Court – with 42 courtrooms (plus seven being built).'

And it is this power which is behind 'Christian' Portugal in her colonial wars.* But before analysis it should be explained why the leaders of the 'free world' not only condone this situation but actively cooperate with the regime in South Africa. The explanation is a simple one and lies in one fact – South Africa's black forced labour

Thanks to this forced labour – the cheapest in the world – investments result in quick and very high profits. Rates of return on American direct investments in South Africa average roughly 19 per cent per annum – against an average return on similar foreign investments of no more than

11 per cent. (US investments in Africa have grown by more than 200 per cent since 1959 and a significantly larger proportion of all US holdings are now in Africa.) The OAU Secretariat lists* the following as the main US banks which are 'actively helping the *apartheid* economy': Bank of America (National Trust and Savings Association), Chase Manhattan Bank, First National City, Manufacturers Hanover Trust Company, Morgan Guaranty Trust Company, Chemical Bank, New York Trust Company, Bankers' Trust Company, Irving Trust Company, Continental Illinois Bank and Trust Company, First National Bank (Chicago). British earnings on direct investment in South Africa are equally remarkable – annual earnings exceed those on investments in other countries by a very comfortable margin. Mining investments in South Africa had a yield of over 30 per cent in 1960.

All this is well detailed in a 100-page UN study – *Industrialization, foreign capital and forced labour in South Africa* – by the well-known expert on South African economy, Sean Gervasi.* Because Western countries who trade with South Africa try their best to hide this traffic, trade statistics are becoming increasingly hard to get hold of and no figures on foreign investments in South Africa have been published for many years. South Africa is, however, one of the most important outlets for British direct overseas investments. Approximately 10 per cent of total British direct investments are in South Africa, only Australia and Canada ranking higher in importance among countries in which British companies invest directly. By 1965 direct investments in South Africa exceeded those in the USA and they were only slightly less than total direct British investments in India and Malaysia combined.*

Against this background it must be recognised that Southern Africa is riddled with wars and ugly racial tensions which threaten more conflicts of a horrible nature. The Liberation Movements from the Portuguese

Colonies have already established a tradition of a 'non-racialist' war; guerillas are permanently told by their political officers that they are not fighting 'Portugal or the Portuguese' but 'Colonialism', and while progress is made, it is a very long and slow process – inevitably. But how long will other African leaders – the Nyereres and particularly the Kaundas – be able to maintain this line? And what of the African masses in Zimbabwe (Rhodesia), Namibia (South-West Africa) and South Africa?

Yet, all this seems to be of no avail and the 'free world' is entering 1974 with a firm stake in a Southern Africa more and more under the control of South Africa.

This was well supported by an analysis of the situation in that part of the world, which appeared in mid-summer 1971 in the authoritative *The Round Table – The Commonwealth Journal of International Affairs.** In an article entitled 'South Africa's Forward Policy in Africa – Milestones on the Great North Road', Robert Molteno wrote:

Disillusion was perhaps the keynote to African events in the sixties. It has grown among various sections of the states' populations – civil servants resenting political control, farmers disappointed in their hopes of rapidly rising standards of living, opposition politicians suffering under authoritarian measures. External observers have also become disillusioned. Liberals in Britain are disappointed at the decline of parliamentary democracy in Africa. Radicals are dismayed at the conservatism of the new elites. Political scientists feel that Africa is characterised by institutionless disorders. Several Western governments, notably Mr Heath's new Tory Administration, have become increasingly irritated by the persistent rhetoric of African states on colonialism and racialism in Southern Africa, and cynical too about the continent's capacity to match that rhetoric with meaningful action.

But there is at least one exception to the general pessimism, and that is the South African Government. Today the mood in the Ministry of Foreign Affairs at Pretoria is one of soaring self-confidence. This self-confidence is compounded of several elements: for one thing, White South Africans believe that sectional conflicts in Africa have demonstrated the validity of the apartheid tenet that new states which disregard pre-colonial political boundaries are not viable. Also, Western disillusion with Black Africa *pari passu* means a less critical eye being cast on South Africa. Thus it appears that the Republic is within sight of being 'over the hump' in its struggle to turn back the tide of international criticism and pressure, and in particular to overcome the hostility of Black Africa. The key to this latter prospect has been the outward looking foreign policy she has pursued with such success in the past four years.

This analysis, describing with accuracy the mood of the West towards Africa, further stressed the predominant role of Pretoria in Southern Africa, by adding: 'Clearly, South Africa is militarily preponderant, economically involved and politically active in the sub-continent today in a way that was undreamed of ten years ago.' It then drove to the heart of the matter by asking: 'What then are the interests propelling South Africa on her new thrust into Africa?' And answered by pointing out that South Africa considers herself threatened not by the established African governments, like Zambia or Tanzania, but by Liberation Movements, particularly those of the Portuguese colonies which are pursuing the struggle with greater assurance than before.

The South African Government dare not allow these wars to reach her territory. For they would disrupt the economy, make it easier for liberation movements to recruit and shatter Western businessmen's image of

South Africa as a stable state – and it is this image which accounts for the continuing flow of Western investment ... which is so essential to the Republic's balance of payments and which also accounts for the reluctance of the West to support the freedom struggle. ... South Africa cannot now afford to allow liberation movements to win even in the Portuguese colonies [on which] she will become by the late 1970s significantly dependent ... the stated Portuguese intention of settling one million Portuguese colonists in the lower Zambezi (the Cabora Bassa project) and half a million more in Southern Angola (the Cunene project) would, if fulfilled over the next decade or so, immeasurably strengthen white South Africa.

These considerations have compelled South Africa to aid the anti-liberation forces beyond her borders.

Clearly, it is because Portugal can no longer assume, by herself, the defence of her colonies and, unforeseen events aside, NATO cannot further increase its assistance to colonial wars without repercussions elsewhere, that South Africa is stepping in. In other words, one has to look at this Portuguese inability to maintain her colonies in order to understand the whys and wherefores of South Africa's thrust northwards which Pretoria describes as 'The Outward Looking Policy', the 'fruitful economic co-operation with the developing countries, especially with African countries', the 'non-aggression treaties with African states' or, finally, the 'dialogue'.

The map on page 32 shows the zone of Southern Africa which Pretoria wants to include within its sphere of influence or – *lebensraum*. The only forces which today stand against this thrust on the Great North Road are the MPLA and the FRELIMO and also, indirectly but significantly, the distant PAIGC.

In midsummer 1971, following the fall of President Obote in Uganda, plots to overthrow first President

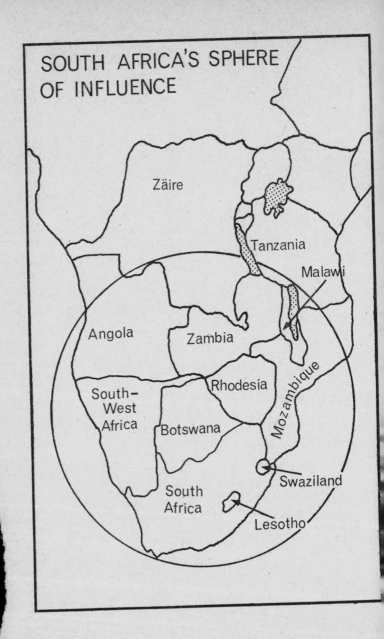

SOUTH AFRICA'S SPHERE OF INFLUENCE

Zäire

Tanzania

Malawi

Angola

Zambia

South-West Africa

Rhodesia

Mozambique

Botswana

Swaziland

South Africa

Lesotho

Kaunda and then President Nyerere were engineered by Pretoria but their real targets were not the two presidents so much as the FRELIMO and the MPLA, whose only sanctuary is Zambia.

The attempts to invade the Republic of Guinea – engineered and conducted by Portuguese using anti-Sékou Touré dissident Guineans as is now widely recognised – showed that the offices of the PAIGC, and Amilcar Cabral himself, were the main targets. Events also showed that PAIGC elements were instrumental in repulsing the invaders. The Pretoria plot calls for different tactics in Southern Africa, but there is little doubt that should events in Guinea Republic repeat themselves in Zambia or Tanzania, MPLA and FRELIMO would play an even greater role than the PAIGC in Conakry.

But let us first look at the cost of the colonial wars to Portugal – which explains why Lisbon can only play second fiddle to South Africa in her own 'Overseas Territories'.

At What Cost Portugal's Colonial Wars?

FOR the first time since war broke out in Angola ten years ago, the Portuguese budget for 1971 was not to give first priority to defence alone; the Law of Ways and Means approved by the National Assembly that year gave first priority to national defence *and* to public investments envisaged under the Third National Development Plan.

The 1971 extraordinary budget provides 7,030·6 million escudos for defence and security expenditures – an increase of 10·5 per cent over the previous year. Expenditures for defence and security during the period 1965-8 rose by more than 50 per cent, or nearly twice the budgetary increase in normal government expenditures. While the ordinary budget* has risen by 39 per cent from 1968-71, that of defence and security has risen by less than 25 per cent. This trend was in fact offset by a simultaneous and sharp increase, between 1967 and 1970, in military expenditures in the colonies; military allocations in Angola alone more than doubled. In Mozambique, the air force budget rose by almost 50 per cent and that of the navy by 25 per cent. In Guinea Bissao, increases were approximately 100 per cent for the navy, 85 per cent for the air force and 30 per cent for the army.

During the same period, the ratio of total military expenditures in the colonies to that of Portugal herself rose from 29 per cent in 1967 to 47 per cent in 1970.

In the 1971 budget, the main items of military expenditures were: extraordinary overseas military forces – 4,000 million escudos; extraordinary re-equipment of army and air force – 1,617.3 million escudos; and the purchase of naval units – 640 million escudos. These, according to the Defence Minister, allowed Portugal to 'double' its helicopter fleet (with French helicopters) over the past year.

No official information is available on actual defence expenditures in 1969 and 1970. It is only known that, in 1970, the original budgetary allocation was 6,349.9 million escudos, to which several supplementary allocations were made afterwards, including 1,500 million escudos in March 1970 for re-equipment of army and air force; 1,800 million escudos in June; 129.2 million escudos in August; 47.4 million escudos in September and 105.4 million escudos in October – all for the *Forças Militares Extraodinarias do Ultramar*.

In 1968, of a total budget expenditure of 23,193.3 million escudos, 11,162.9 million escudos went to defence of which 10,696.6 million escudos for military defence proper and 466,300 escudos for security. A calculation made by the UN* showed that, more extraordinary than for a poor country like Portugal to have spent (in 1968) 42 per cent of her total public expenditures for wars, was the fact that for every one hundred escudos spent on ordinary government services* another seventy-nine escudos were spent on military purposes!

organisation of the army was also reshaped; seven Military Regions (five in Portugal and one each in Angola and Mozambique) and eight Independent Territorial Commands were created. The Angola Military Region (HQ in Luanda) was divided into five Territorial Commands – Cabinda, the north, central, south and eastern commands with HQs at Carmaona, Nova Lisboa, Sa da Bandeira and Luso.

The Military Region of Mozambique was divided into three Independent Territorial Commands – north (Nampula), south (Beira), and central (Lourenço Marques).

Troops in the field were also reorganised and, in addition to the *Forças militares extraordinarias no ultramar* (the Overseas Extraordinary Expeditionary Corps from Portugal), local armies known as 'Normal Garrison Troops' and 'Reinforcement Troops' were established within the *Forças Armadas*. The 'Garrison Troops' were given the task of preventing enemy penetration, defending strategic points and communication lines, obtaining military intelligence and cooperating with local civilian authorities and conducting psychological warfare. They would also support the *unidades de intervençao* – the combat troops. A series of new measures characterised the para-military groups which according to Portuguese legislation became *Forças Militarizadas* – Militarised Forces. These could be divided into two groups, one more to do with security and the whites, and the other with native troops. Three different types of African units were created: *Tropas Especiais (TEs)*, *Grupos Especiais (GEs)* and the *Flechas*. While the G.E.s possess simple military training,* the TEs and the *Flechas* participate in military actions to protect the flanks of the white Portuguese troops and penetrate the bush. The *Flechas* are known to be used by the DGS for security operations. They are exempt from tax. White para-military forces include the OPVDC – the Provincial Organisation of Volunteers and Civil Defence – which trains the GEs. There is the Rural

Guard, composed mainly of Europeans, and very much feared by the local population, and the *Agentes Passivos*, the Militia and the Railway Brigades. The most distinguished bodies to be included in the *Forças Militarizadas* are the Public Security Police – *Policia de Segurença Publica* (PSP) – and the DGS, the former PIDE. Of the 3,027 men strong PIDE, 1,116 were in Angola and 665 in Mozambique*

This streamlining of the forces which are to achieve in the Colonies the 'return' of the *Paz Portuguesa** included on 3 April 1970, an allocation of three million escudos to the 18·3 million escudos already allocated that year in Mozambique for expenditure on prisons. In Angola, in March 1971, 100 million escudos were allocated for the construction of new prison facilities.

Rather like France during the Algerian war, Portugal is waging war on two levels. The first is purely military, which she could not maintain without the help of her NATO allies. The second is a psychological war waged inside the colonies, which aims simultaneously at redistributing the native population, in order to remove it from contact with the forces of liberation, and at settling more colonists, with a view to eventually establishing a new thesis of 'autonomy of the Overseas Territories' (such a project was outlined by Marcelo Caetano on 2 December 1970 in Parliament).

We have seen the cost of the colonial wars to Portugal – efforts to modernise the armed forces have only increased this cost. Portugal's military budget is today a far cry from what it was in the early sixties when Portuguese troops in the colonies numbered only 20,000 men.

Today the Portuguese government has had to mobilise some 150,000 men for the army, 17,500 men for the air force and 15,000 men for the navy. There are 2,500 marines, and members of the *Forças Militarizadas* may well number over 50,000 men. Various sources* put the total strength of the Portuguese Armed Forces at 180,000 men.

According to the Portuguese *Revista de Marinha** in July 1971 the Portuguese fleet consisted of 163 ships – 104 of them in Portuguese 'territories'. Half of them, mainly the smaller ships, were in Guinea. Only three frigates supplied under US aid were assigned within the 'NATO' framework in Europe. Thirty ships have been provided by the NATO countries – West Germany 11, France 8, USA 7, UK 4.

The Portuguese Air Force, equipped by the same countries and Italy, maintains its best units in the colonies.*

Already in 1967, as a result of the extent of the struggles for liberation, the Salazar government had increased the strength of the army by 25 per cent. Mobilisable reserves amount to 500,000 men. This represents, more or less, the limit of the country's capacity for mobilisation; in Portugal men may be called up until the age of forty-five. Compulsory military service was increased to four years in 1967. Recently the government ordered the remobilisation of the four preceding classes for a period of two years.

Only the bodies of officers are returned to Portugal to their families for burial, all the rest are buried on the spot in the colonies. Bodies are returned to Portugal during night-time only and when the list of dead officers is too long it appears in instalments in the 'Army information' column of the Lisbon dailies. Officially, there are over 20,000 war cripples.

According to a compilation based on official communiqués alone, Portuguese losses in Africa are proportionately higher than those of other publicised colonial wars in the recent past involving France or Britain.* The total is 4,028 for the three territories and there is an average of 240 deaths per annum to be added to those wounded who died in hospital. This figure, the study goes on to say, would amount to a total of 1,920 deaths in eight years on average, bringing the overall total of those dead either in combat or in consequence of combat wounds to approximately 5,800. If one took into account as valid the average of one accidental death for every three deaths in combat – as happened during the Algerian war – the overall total Portuguese dead in the colonial wars would near the figure of 6,800. This would constitute an average of nearly a thousand a year, which is a very high proportion for a total population, in 1971, of 8,600,000.*

In 1967, the army had to admit that, out of 80,000 men called up, 14,000 were evading their obligations, and that clandestine emigration of young Portuguese to France alone, between 1962 and 1966, exceeded the number of Portuguese who settled in the colonies during the same period.

But three years later, in 1970, the admission became more alarming. A confidential report of the Portuguese General Staff* stated:

The proliferation of anti-government organisations and the agitation that they create, leads to an unsuitable psychological climate which, by affecting the activities of students, affects the country, which seems troubled and does not know what to do to lead its children back to the right path ... In the metropolis generally, the population continues to show little interest in the war overseas and ignores the efforts being made by the armed forces. The student masses remain highly vulnerable to pacifist propaganda ...

The working masses, ignoring great national problems, let themselves be easily led by the propaganda oriented towards demanding better wages and living conditions. The most advanced groups continue to be the hot beds of subversion and the groups which are springing up have proved highly effective.

Overseas, in a general way, the native populations continue to tend towards subversion, especially when they have strength, or when geographic conditions make actions by our troops difficult or impossible. The indigenous population on the periphery of the largest urban centres, generally detribalised, continue to show themselves as very susceptible to enemy propaganda. The European population continues to demonstrate overt support for the war, but only cooperates against subversion when its material interests are directly in danger.

The psychological situation is precarious, in the metropolis as well as overseas.

This state of affairs has inevitably created a crisis, which is reflected in the existence inside Portugal herself of a silent but growing opposition to the colonial wars.

Inevitably, the Portuguese soldiers in the colonies show little enthusiasm – except specialised units like the parachutists. As for the native soldiers, they too are posing problems – as has been the case with all colonial troops, particularly when having to fight independence movements within their own country; a tiny fraction turns traitor, another secretly cooperates with the resistance and the bulk remains passive but potentially ready to turn its guns against the colonial master.

Since 1967/8, Portuguese officered Angolan soldiers are no longer used to execute their compatriots as they refuse to carry out such duties. The Portuguese Air Force used, traditionally, to recruit a number of educated natives every year (15 from Guinea Bissao, 20 from Angola and 40-50 from Mozambique) to serve as radio operators, mechanics, etc. These were prize situations and there were more volunteers than vacancies. Starting mid-1968, there were few volunteers and Portuguese authorities are now unable to find candidates from the colonies in sufficient numbers.

Militarily, Portugal entered the year 1972 on the defensive practically everywhere in the colonies. On 8 July 1970, the *New York Times* reported that Portuguese officers in Angola 'no longer talked of winning'. Offensive actions, notably in Mozambique, were also for defensive purposes – namely to prevent FRELIMO sabotage of the Cabora Bassa Dam; and also to prevent FRELIMO elements, having advanced from Tanzania and Zambia, to join in central Mozambique south of Malawi. The forces in the Tete Province, which had originally infiltrated from Zambia, had crossed the Zambezi – a natural barrier the Portuguese General Staff was sure FRELIMO would never have been able to cross. As for the FRELIMO forces which had originally come from Zambia, they already had elements beyond the third Portuguese defence line – one going from Nacala on the sea to Malawi in the vicinity of Amaramba. The first Portuguese defence line had been the border with Tanzania and the second between Porto Amelia on the east and Vila Cabral, on the west, near Malawi.

The main Portuguese effort, very much under the influence of lessons believed to have been learnt from the Vietnam war, had gone into air attacks followed by ground operations; a zone would be bombed and strafed for several hours by aircraft, then helicopters would bring in troops while garrisons – in most cases already besieged – would make sorties.

Guerillas have to walk hundreds of kilometres and each man carries up to twenty kilos weight. In Angola, guerillas have been obliged to carry less ammunition and more food – for both themselves and the civilian populations – since the Portuguese resorted to chemical warfare with the aim of starving out the populations in liberated areas and making the MPLA's task harder.

Portugal resorted to chemical warfare for the first time on 1 May 1970, when planes, flying low over the banks of the Luena River, in eastern Angola, started spraying cassava fields. The use of chemical agents by Portugal in Angola is now an internationally accepted fact. *The Times* of London, on 11 December 1970, had already stated that 'The United States has indications that Portugal has used herbicides to destroy rebel food crops in Angola according to State Department officials'.

Guerrilhero* reported that 'in 1969 US exports of herbicides to Portugal were valued at 57,330 dollars for the whole year. In the first 11 months of 1970 exports of herbicides already amounted to 229,320 dollars. The US denies that these are going to Angola – but isn't it a strange coincidence that it was in May 1970 that MPLA began to report Portuguese use of herbicides in Angola? Companies exporting these products include Dow Chemicals, Agrisect Chemicals (New York), Hercules Inc. (Wilmington, Delaware), Monsanto Inc. (St Louis), and US Rubber Co. (Naugatuck, Connecticut).'

An official Zambian document,* addressed to UN Secretary General of the UN Conference on the Human Environment, Mr Maurice Strong, stated: '... Products thus being sprayed over liberated zones proved to be herbicides and defoliants of the following nature, according to the Sam (Servicio de Assistencia Medica – of the MPLA): 2,4-D (dichlorophenoxyacetic acid); 2,4,5-T (trichlorophenoxyacetic acid); cacodylic acid and picloram (from Dow Chemical Co., with the commercial name of Tordon).'

Following repercussions in the international press* the Portuguese stopped using chemical agents in Angola in the latter part of 1971. Claims by PAIGC that the Portuguese intended resorting to chemical warfare in Guinea Bissao, may well indicate that the interruption of this type of war in Angola is only temporary. As a matter of fact, the *Sunday Times* of 9 July 1972 was to disclose that during the two weeks ending 17 April of that year, at least six aeroplanes manned by South African pilots had undertaken a secret defoliation operation in northern Mozambique, obviously to relieve guerilla pressure in the Cabora Bassa region. The *Sunday Times* said that the pilots were South African 'mercenaries' flying for the Portuguese Air Force, but it is more likely that it was an act of close cooperation between Portuguese and South African forces, and still further evidence of the increased interference on the part of the latter in Portugal's African wars. The *Sunday Times* further revealed that British Petroleum, 48·4% owned by the UK government, was helping the South African state-dominated chemical giant Sentrachem to manufacture Convolvotox, a mixture containing 2,4-D which not only kills broad-leafed plants but can also inhibit fertilisation. Shell also has links with Sentrachem. B.P., whose Portuguese subsidiary is the *Companhia Portuguesa dos Petroleos B.P.*, boasts, ironically enough, of an 'Environment Committee'!

South Africa, as we have already seen, has her own 'sphere of influence' – or *Lebensraum*. As for Portugal, what she wants her *Paz Portuguesa* for, is to achieve her '*espaco nacional*' – but it is a very costly ambition, well beyond the means of a poor little country.

'The Border of Human Decency'

'THIS is the border of human decency!'*

The Swedish government is not the only one in Western Europe to have realised this 'border'. Denmark and Norway officially objected to the fact that the June 1971 NATO Ministerial Conference took place in Portugal 'whose political line is not in accordance with the principles and aims of the Charter of the United Nations'.*

To other western governments, the British Tory one in particular, the 'border' is somewhere else – it lies with profit. The influence of the business lobbies in the Rhodesian 'settlement', which a leading British weekly editorially labelled 'An Ignoble End to Empire',* was only too evident; the fact that the rule of an oppressive white minority regime had been consolidated and the inevitable future consequences this was bound to bring out – including those in the economic field – were almost instantly forgotten in favour of calculations as to what effects the unloading of Rhodesia's stockpiled tobacco would have on the markets, and the reopening of English and other markets to Rhodesia now that sanctions had been lifted.

The accent on 'business' which characterised the whole western attitude in this problem, was further illustrated by a US Congress decision, while Anglo-Rhodesian negotiations were in course, that the US would resume its purchases of chrome from Rhodesia in defiance of the UN Security Council Sanctions against the illegal regime of Salisbury. While dockers went on strike in protest against the arrival of the first shipload of Rhodesian chrome, Senator Edward Kennedy said that the ship would be unloading 'a tremendous cargo of American discredit'.

The September 1970 issue of the *Standard Bank Review* published a supplement on Angola and Mozambique which read:

... up to a few years ago few people outside Portugal and
its colonies had any intimate knowledge of Angola. To
most it was merely a country situated somewhere in
Africa. Today the situation is very different. Interest in
the progress of this country is becoming widespread in
business, financial and mining circles, particularly those
in South Africa, and South African capital is starting to
flow north.

On 30 November 1970 the *New York Times* carried a
two-page advertisement on Angola, to attract new foreign
investments. One comment on the Benguela Railway,
whose full name incidentally is the 'Benguela Railway
Company of the United Kingdom', read: 'The railway is
one of the most profitable in the world. It has an average
annual profit of about $10 million.'

On 19 July 1971, the *Financial Times* published a special
survey on Angola and Mozambique in which a half-page
advertisement on Cabora Bassa – 'the greatest source of
power in the African Continent' – read: 'Portuguese Africa
Is Booming'. *The Times* of 17 June 1972, in a special
supplement on Portugal, published an advertisement quot-
ing 'Social and Cultural Progress' in Angola by the
Diamond Company, Diamang. One should nevertheless
mention still another supplement in *The Times*, of 17
February 1973, concerning Mozambique, with such
appetising headlines as 'A Territory on the Move', 'The
Sound of Boom!', 'Transport to Success', 'The Paradise',
etc. Yet, for some time West German firms working for the
Cabora Bassa scheme had been besieging Bonn authorities
for insurance against war risks. Such examples of overt
western business interest in racialist and colonial Southern
Africa can be cited *ad nauseam*.

Western politics in Southern Africa are essentially
geared to serve such business interests. France is for the
'dialogue' between Pretoria and whatever independent
African state is willing to play this game, for no other

reason than her economic interests. So is Western Germany and, in April 1972, it was disclosed, in the Roman press, that Italian fascists were, together with the Greek colonels, financing their activities in Europe through the illegal trade in arms with South Africa, Rhodesia and Portugal. The same Italian fascists had revived the old Mussolini dream of an Italian colony in Angola by transferring to this country Italian settlers who could no longer stay in Somalia. But it is British policies in Southern Africa which attract the most attention.

Because Britain has been for so long the dominant power in Southern Africa, and because she maintains in her former territories powerful economic interests and has a particular relationship with her 'oldest ally', Portugal, who still occupies large portions of this part of the world, it is impossible not to speak of her responsibilities in Southern Africa. In a sense these responsibilities are greater since America has not openly taken over from Britain there as it did elsewhere in the world and Washington intentionally remains in the political backstage of Southern Africa. This does not mean of course that the USA is dormant.*

The USSR can be said to be largely absent from the political scene in Southern Africa and, while China has a more active policy there, stories of 'deep Chinese penetration' belong more to the domain of fantasy.

In the early seventies, the British attitude towards Southern Africa bore the inescapable imprint of Prime Minister Edward Heath. Mr Heath's new Tory administration, as rightly pointed out in *The Commonwealth Journal of International Affairs* mentioned earlier, has become 'increasingly irritated' and 'cynical' about the capabilities of 'African states', implying mainly Tanzania and Zambia.

That Mr Heath was predisposed to feel 'irritated' and 'cynical' about Africans like Nyerere and Kaunda, is only too well known. For Mr Heath belongs to a class of English-

men who this author at least wrongly believed had dis-
appeared with the Suez War fiasco.

The British stand on Pretoria's policy of expansion –
which Whitehall must know quite well – appears distinctly
from Britain's attitudes and actions. Nowhere, neither at
the UN, nor in the field, has Mr Heath shown that he is
opposed to this policy. On the contrary he has gone a long
way to reverse the stand of the preceding Labour government, to resume arms sales to South Africa and to 'sell out'
Rhodesia. These are episodes too well-known to need elabor-
ation here. There is also the less known British policy in the
Indian Ocean where, the 'Indian Ocean Soviet threat' can
be said to have been started more by Mr Heath than by the
Red Fleet itself. Mr Heath initiated the 'Indian Ocean
Soviet threat' because he was more pre-occupied with its
South African implications and his strong desire to resume
arms sales to South Africa. The Tory administration, which
is motivated by 'business at any cost', had in fact found a
handy pretext to resume arms sales to Pretoria. On 2 February 1972, the State Department announced that it was
in contact with the Soviet Union within view of reaching
an agreement whereby both parties would reduce their
naval strength in the Indian Ocean and the Persian Gulf.
This left Mr Heath very much as the sole champion of the
Western cause in the Indian Ocean! But perhaps Mr Heath
was not entirely alone, as now France decided to send a
naval force to the Indian Ocean.* It was clear that this
show of the *tricolore*, too, was not of a nature to deter a
Soviet threat, if any, but that it was more concerned with
the arms sale to South Africa and increasing internal
troubles in Madagascar, where France then had a naval
base at Diego Suarez. Only a few days earlier, on 29 January, the President of the Republic of South Africa, J. J.
Fouché, had stated that 'the protection of the Cape Sea
route and Southern Africa against communist domination'
called for 'other countries' (i.e. other than South Africa and

the UK) to participate in the regular naval exercises held under the Simonstown agreement.

What has never been said to this day, in the British press,* is the fact that at the 1971 Singapore Commonwealth Conference both Presidents Kaunda and Nyerere and President Obote – who was to be overthrown while returning from Singapore to Kampala – tacitly agreed that Britain could have a base on Mauritius, where the Royal Navy continues to keep a naval communications centre. But Mr Heath did not adopt the idea, for his conception of security in the Indian Ocean was bent on resuming the profitable arms sales to Pretoria.

One reason Mr Heath is known to have turned down Mauritius' offer of a naval base, is that Britain did not have the money. Instead, Britain lent the island of Diego Garcia to the Americans, and it can be disclosed that work on the Diego Garcia base began secretly in July 1971 when some one thousand American military personnel disembarked there with bulldozers and other equipment.

Another reason is Mr Heath's almost pathological dislike of Presidents Kaunda and Nyerere. This attitude of personal vengeance was further evidenced when it became known, at the end of January 1972, that on the specific request of the British government, the World Bank had stopped a £4,300,000 loan through its International Development Association for a vital tea development programme in Tanzania, which would allow thousands of peasants living at the subsistence level to move into a cash economy.

Mr Heath never approached his Commonwealth partners of Tanzania and Kenya to propose a joint defence agreement, for both these African countries are also interested in Indian Ocean security; his mind was set on the Simonstown naval base agreement with South Africa and the perspective of British dockyards (instead of French ones) producing warships for Pretoria.

The hallmark of Mr Heath's foreign policy is a brusque take-it-or-leave-it unsentimental realism in which British interests (as the Government interprets them) are put, Palmerston-style, unashamedly first. This real-politik has led the Prime Minister into some uncomfortable postures. It has, for instance, left him facing it out with the leaders of the black Commonwealth, because of his willingness to sell arms to South Africa, and giving the impression that he was even prepared to see the Commonwealth break up rather than shift his own position – presumably on the grounds that if the Commonwealth could break up so easily it was not worth too much worry. Now Mr Heath and Lord Carrington have applied the same approach to Malta, and this time there is to be a parting of the ways.... Mr Heath and Lord Carrington have, however, done the right thing in not being frightened by Reds in the Med – which makes it even odder that they should have been prepared to pay so dear in terms of Commonwealth amity allegedly for fear of Reds in the Indian Ocean.*

Africans will be understood if they return the compliment and they, too, feel 'irritated' and 'cynical' about Mr Heath and his administration.

Despite her military power, the *apartheid* regime has its vulnerable points too, and could be considerably shaken if, for example, the Zulu workers imitated their brethren from Ovamboland and went on strike *en masse*. Such an eventuality, of course, would not cancel the fact that the backbone of *apartheid* is constituted by a lot of diehards* who will only be dislodged by force. It is not irrelevant to stress here, that the inevitability of violence in South Africa is such that even as moderate a figure as the Bishop of Zululand was quoted in *The Times* of 17 May 1972 as saying 'that the harshness of discrimination made a black man look simple and naïve if he continued to advocate the effectiveness of non-violence ... few whites in South Africa were committed to non-violence and there was no reason why there should be any more extensive commitment among blacks'.

Nonetheless, South Africa has to act like a person who knows that, in the long run, she will be cornered and she is acting along two lines accordingly – increase her military power and conduct her foreign policy more along a pattern of plots, by taking advantage of the current isolated position of President Nyerere and President Kaunda in particular, and act before it is too late with regard to the FRELIMO and the MPLA which threaten her Mozambican and Angolan buffer states.

The announcement that French Mirage III and F.1 jets are to be built in South Africa on licence led the *Sunday Times** to consider this new aspect of the close-working military partnership between Pretoria and Paris as a 'prelude' to a 'master-plan', still in its formative stages, to establish a dominant power bloc in Africa. This attempt to create a 'defence pact in Southern Africa' with the inclusion of Rhodesia, Portugal, Malawi, Madagascar, Lesotho, Swaziland and Botswana – under South African leadership – had the blessing of France.

The supreme ambition of the Defence Force diehards, is to possess the atom bomb. In the summer of 1970, Premier Vorster disclosed that work had already started on building a pilot plant to produce enriched uranium, which would make South Africa 'the West's fourth atomic power'. The British author Richard West suggests in a study of the Rio Tinto-Zinc British mining corporation which cooperates with the Pretoria government, that the Rossing mine, located in Namibia, will provide South Africa with the means to make nuclear weapons.* *Le Monde* of 12 February 1972, confirmed by *The Times* of 20 August 1973, spoke of a new method found in South Africa, about which nothing is known, to enrich uranium. Israel is reported to be cooperating with South Africa on atomic matters.

A word should be said here about Israel, which does not

publicly rate as a main supplier of arms to South Africa.
Because Israel has a vast programme of technical assistance
in Africa, where she also cultivates profitable commercial
and economic relations, she has displayed the greatest skill*
in hiding much of her relationship with South Africa,
which can go a long sentimental way, if one remembers
that some leading Israeli personalities have family connections in South Africa – they include the Foreign Minister
Abba Eban and General Mordechai Hod, Head of the
Israel Air Force, who on the occasion of a visit to South
Africa in September 1967, lectured student officers of the
South African Air Force college at Voortrekkhoogte on the
tactics his airmen used in the Middle East. It may well be
that such visitors account in part, for South African threats
of 'Israeli-like raids' against Zambia. Stella Levy, a colonel
in the Israeli army, went to South Africa in 1970 to give a
series of lectures on 'counter-insurrection' and to recruit
female South Africans of Jewish descent for the Israeli
army. It is also worth noting that Israel, which has gone to
such lengths to catch up with former Nazi criminals all
over the world, is remarkably inactive about such of these
people who are known to have found haven in South Africa
and Namibia.

The celebrated Israeli sub-machine gun, Uzi, is manufactured under licence – transacted through Belgium – in
South Africa, and according to a statement made by the
Director of Israel's military industries, on 10 December
1970, South Africa headed the list of clients for Israeli
armament, whose exports had increased five times in 1970,
compared to 1967. There is little doubt that, taking advantage of the arms embargo decreed by the UN against South
Africa, Israel must have increased her arms sales to Pretoria. According to *Le Monde* Israeli exports to South
Africa increased from $3 million in 1969 to $10 million in
1970 and they would reach $20 million in 1973.* Israel's
new sea–sea Gabriel missile is believed to have been sold to
South Africa; there are reports of cooperation in the atomic

field, and this author has reliably learned that, in case of necessity, the South African Air Force would have recourse to Israeli pilots to handle its French-built Mirages. For, however strange it may sound, as I write this South Africa does not have enough pilots of her own to handle all the Mirages she possesses, and the few suitable candidate pilots for these planes had been lured, by better pay, to the SAA. In 1970 and 1971 a few South African pilots had a mad time in trying to keep in the air a large number of Mirages to prevent them from being grounded.

What is South Africa building up all this armament for? There is, of course, the good excuse of the Soviet or Chinese threats, but even before any representative of Mao had set foot in Africa *apartheid* and its logic were at work.

An official South African publication, *The Concept of Economic Cooperation in Southern Africa,** and much more explicitly another book, *The Third Africa,** provide fascinating reading. Under a pseudo-economic terminology they unveil the whole domineering strategy of *apartheid*, the steps South Africa is to take to maintain herself by creating a zone of economic and political dominance. A circle on the official South African map we reproduce on page 32 shows the border of this sphere of influence.

The strategy behind this grand scheme was popularised in May 1969 in the South African *Financial Gazette*:

> The best way in which we can neutralize the efforts by the Anti-Apartheid Movements, SANROC, the Afro-Asian Block in the United Nations, to isolate and under-mine South Africa's safety is to make a diplomatic break-through in Africa.

> If South Africa could gain the support of a number of African States, these enemy groups would be left without a cause and the Republic's international position would improve drastically.

> These movements should in the first instance not be fought in London, New York or other World cities, but

in Africa. *Africa is South Africa's passport to success in the international world.*

The *Report from South Africa** which is distributed by the South African Foundation had this to say:

Decolonisation has left a vacuum in Black Africa which South Africa is *quietly moving out to fill.* South Africans are playing an important role as expatriate experts vital in the newly independent nations. Their companies are busy in such lands as Malawi and Mozambique. Their money is financing the projects. *And their intelligence men are building a chain of listening posts across the continent.**

But perhaps matters were stated most convincingly in *The Third Africa* which said:

On its part South Africa dominates 'The Third Africa'* to the same if not a greater extent that the United States enjoys pre-eminence in the Americas and so, very much like the US with the CIA and all, in the Southern hemisphere of America, South Africa conducts her 'plots' in Southern Africa.

Late in 1970, in State House Lusaka, this author was speaking to President Kaunda – the Zambian leader who knew then of the plot to silence him. Events followed in quick succession, and this author remembers another conversation – in State House, Dar es Salaam, in May 1971. President Nyerere had felt worried enough about the situation in the sister Republic of Zambia, to send his Special Assistant B. Munanka to Lusaka that very next morning. The outline of the plot, which was well under way, had already been brought to public attention in a Tanzanian daily, *The Standard,** entitled 'The Pattern of Strangulation Engulfs Africa' – in a remarkable political analysis the author said:

... The road that Mwalimu Nyerere has chosen for his

people is that of non-alignment. But today we see the horrible truth ... that it is a path beset with enormous difficulties ... one that ... is not favoured by the major powers. The way of the West, and especially the US is to assume that those who are not with them are against them. That is why the people of Indo-China have been given the choice of Western domination or death.

Much the same thing is happening in Africa, but in a more subtle fashion. The ideal of African unity is slowly but surely being eroded and those countries which value their independence ... are being isolated.

It is abundantly clear that the pressure is on to force Tanzania to toe the western line ...

With the OAU in apparent disarray ... it came as no surprise that Britain's decision to sell arms to South Africa brought only a muted response from the free nations of Africa.

Knowing the political chaos caused by the Uganda coup, Prime Minister Heath felt safe to make his announcement. And if he expected little reaction, he got what he expected.

What brought about this sudden change of stance, this lowering of voices by Africa's leaders? Was it the Uganda coup alone? Hardly, for it seems there are other, more powerful influences at work.

It is common knowledge, for instance, that Zambia is experiencing a series of internal and external problems not the least of which is the sudden drop of copper prices on the world market. This sudden, downward fluctuation is reminiscent, in a sinister way, of the collapse of sisal prices following nationalisation of the industry in Tanzania.

There are also reports of tribal and factional differences within Zambia and of a serious food shortage in some parts of the country. These reports are not to be doubted, because Zambia has openly admitted that she is buying maize to help offset famine.

Subtle pressures on Tanzania also are evident, like the

decision by major shipping lines to place a 25 per cent
surcharge on all goods moving through Dar-es-Salaam.

Taken individually, these events may not seem to be
too important. But collectively – and in the light of the
Uganda coup – they form a pattern of strangulation that
seems to be enveloping a whole region of Africa ...

What did President Kaunda already know in late 1970?
That the tactics against him would be economic blockade
harassments by Portugal ... to be followed by South
African offers of economic assistance ... and that while
military intimidations on the borders would take place...
the 'main effort' would be to win over Zambia 'from the
interior' ... by nurturing tribal divisions and in particular
by playing on the weaknesses of the administration formed
by the new national bourgeoisie ...

In early 1971, Zambia was struck by an acute food shortage, due to the Portuguese who almost totally cut the flow
of Zambian imports through the ports of Beira, Nacala and
Lourenço Marques in Mozambique and Lobito in Angola
... Zambia had to go through the humiliation of importing
maize from where it was conveniently available ... from
South Africa and Rhodesia.*

Following the crisis created by the food shortage, and
while internal political quarrels, which we shall deal with
in the next chapter, were under way in Lusaka, there was,
in October, at Mwinilunga (see last chapter in this book) on
Zambia's north-western frontier, a harassment on the
border by the Portuguese. During the same month, in the
south, South African armed police entered Zambian territory, from the strategic Caprivi strip, under the 'law' of
'hot pursuit' – used by the French against Tunisia, at Sakiet
Sidi Youssef, during the Algerian War.

Would increasing Portuguese inability to cope with the
steady advance of nationalist guerillas in Angola and
Mozambique compel Pretoria to act in a more decisive way
before it was too late? In Angola's Kunene region, in-

habited by the Ovambos whose brethren had already rebelled in Namibia, the MPLA had activated a new front known as the 6th Region and in Mozambique FRELIMO activities were closing in on the Cabora Bassa region to the great worry of West German firms involved in the dam project. FRELIMO was furthermore successfully sabotaging Malawi's rail and road connections with Beira and Rhodesia. In a dispatch from Salisbury dated 31 May 1972, the *Financial Times* reported that FRELIMO activities in the Tete Province were 'posing increasingly serious prolems for Rhodesian security forces'. On 8 April, South Africa's Minister of Police S. L. Muller, warned President Kaunda about Pretoria's 'mounting impatience' over the activities of Zambia-based guerillas in the Caprivi strip and a week later thirteen Portuguese aircraft attacked the Tanzanian village of Kitaya.

'Joint operations' – between South Africa, Rhodesia and Portugal – against the MPLA and FRELIMO were decided upon, according to *The Observer* of 29 February 1972, on the occasion of the visit of the rebel Rhodesian Premier Smith to Mr Vorster during that month. Shortly after this visit, the President of the South African Armaments Board, Prof. Samuels, stated on 25 March in a BBC monitored broadcast from Johannesburg, that South Africa 'could not allow Mozambique and Angola to fall because in the struggle against communist influence in Africa, South Africa's northern frontier could be taken as the border of Zaïre across Zambia to Tanzania'. There could be no clearer assertion of the *Lebensraum* policy, but there was equally no indication whatsoever that the Western world was in any way to stand against this blatant intention to now openly violate 'the borders of human decency'.

The West had done its hypocritical best, France in particular, to bring about Voerster's 'master plan' of 'the dialogue'. But, mid-summer 1972, 'the dialogue' was a lame duck. President Houphouet-Boigny found it wiser to keep silent and an even greater advocate of 'the dialogue', Presi-

dent Tsiranana of the Malagasy republic was overthrown.
The 'Madagascar blow' was all the greater in that students
in revolt not only obtained the termination of all forms of
cooperation with Pretoria, but also called for an end to
the French naval base at Diego Suarez. Even more important, they asked for an end to the continued application of
an alien educational system – the French *baccalaureat*.
Chain reaction against *la culture française*, in its traditional colonial form, took place at once elsewhere in franco-
phone Africa.

With even little Lesotho, land-locked within South
Africa, challenging 'the dialogue', the next alternative of
Voerster's 'master plan' was put into action with increasing
urgency – the overthrow of Presidents Kaunda and
Nyerere by any and all means, including assassination,
which would, as in the cases of Cabral and Mondlane, be
carried out by African traitors with 'the long arms' of the
BOSS and DGS close at hand.

Kaunda – so much more vulnerable because of tribal
divisions in Zambia, and because of his copper-spoilt bourgeois administrators – and Nyerere should be replaced by
Banda-like black racialist dictators for there was nothing
that would suit the white racialists better.

With Ian Smith becoming too much of a rebel for
Whitehall, Mr Heath would also prefer a Banda-like solution in Salisbury. The closure of the Rhodesian/Zambian
border by Salisbury in early 1973 backfired, and the blockade in fact proved to be a blessing for Kaunda who decided
to keep the border closed after Ian Smith had reopened it.
It will be revealed one day how much the bourgeois elements of the Zambian Administration tried to convince
Kaunda that he had better continue relying on old colonial
roots rather than accepting the spontaneous Tanzanian
offer, which has made Dar es Salaam virtually a Zambian
port. On 15 March and again on 22 August President
Kaunda warned that under the pretext of attacking
guerilla training camps, South Africans and Rhodesians

would attack Zambian towns and villages.

On 2 September, in an interview with a West German newspaper, Dr Caetano accused Zambia of being the 'pivotal point of unrest' in Portugal's colonies. Information was also at hand indicating that South Africa and Rhodesia would attempt to sabotage and/or raid Dar es Salaam, now the life-line of Mozambique, Zambia and Angola.

The Emergent Black Bourgeois Nationalist Class

A few days before the Lusaka non-aligned summit, President Kaunda held a press interview, which is memorable both for what he said and for its setting.

The décor was that of a simple African hut village, at Mfuwe, in the game reserve of Lunluangwa Valley, to where the President escapes when he can, to rest and reflect; the interviewers were Maria-Antonietta Macciocchi, the well-known Italian journalist and author and the then member of parliament (Communist), the respected French journalist from *Le Monde*, Jacques Nobécourt, and Alberto Jacoviello, of *L'Unita*, and Italy's best foreign policy commentator.*

Doctor Kaunda, a man of a warmth and simplicity which are hard to describe, whose belief in 'humanism' has become his political philosophy, was at his best in this captivating setting in the very heart of Africa.

'I thought I had met a prophet,' Jacoviello was to write.

Talking of how he envisaged the growth of his country, with a perpetual accent on the 'value of man and of his environment' – well before 'environment' became such a fashionable expression in the mouths of politicians – Kaunda said at one point: 'But I have fears that while trying to build up Zambia, I am myself unleashing forces, mainly a class of national bourgeoisie, which will prove more difficult to deal with than the former colonial masters.'

At this point, this author should acknowledge the complete analysis made of President Kaunda by Jacoviello, which would have read: '... a prophet – but a disarmed one'. Jacoviello, a personal friend, deleted these last words from his copy when discussing the interview with this author, who has now to confess that he did not at that time believe that Zambia's well-fed and well-paid emergent bourgeoisie would contribute to weaken its leader so much in such a short time.

The lack of any serious militant past – only a handful really struggled and the rest had their independence granted with the usual British ceremonials – and the 'silver spoon' of Zambian copper have resulted in the majority of educated Zambians looking more for the comforts of life and tragically lacking national and political consciousness. It is this author's conviction that, without Kaunda, this bourgeoisie would easily turn Zambia into 'a Malawi'.

President Nyerere, the real brother-in-arms of Kaunda, knew this only too well and, when addressing a meeting of Zambia's UNIP party at Mulungushi in 1971 he said: 'All they [the neo-colonial forces] need, is to call you *Your Excellencies* ... to get round you.' (Even in Tanzania, where political consciousness is much more developed and the TANU party is much more aware of its role, the *Standard* was to say: 'Ten years after independence, the nation still has among its officials many who are more impressed by business suits and cocktail parties than by production figures.') As a result, Zambian bourgeoisie only pays lip service to the struggle against colonialism and *apartheid*. It proved easier for President Kaunda to pull Italy out of the Cabora Bassa scheme than to make an end to such essential imports as ... Portuguese and South African wine!

However contradictory as this may seem it would suit Pretoria should a black racialist come to power in Zambia – the theory is more difficult to apply in Tanzania where tribalism is on a very low ebb and racialism less flagrant – for, to the master-minds of *apartheid*, the idea would be to have on the one hand white racialists with their black boys, and on the other black racialists with their white boys. Men like Kaunda and Nyerere who believe in multiracialism are dangerous men in the pay of Moscow – or preferably Peking. Two well-known western authors – Leonard Barnes and René Dumont* – have dealt at length with the havoc being created by the African bourgeois classes to the particular detriment of the peasant class. Barnes speaks of 'the politicians and administrators of black African states [who] have degenerated into highly privileged and highly dis-illusioned cliques with no care beyond the material concerns of their own closed shop'. He appropriately goes on to describe how foreign 'aid' resulted mainly in the creation of a parasitic caste of government employees whose overriding ambition is to appropriate for themselves an ever increasing proportion of public revenue. Dumont speaks of 'urban privileged minorities' who have replaced the white colon-iser – of their abusive profits, their total disregard of the public interest, and of their alliance 'with neo-colonialism'.

The same emergent African bourgeois classes are to be found in power over practically all Africa, which explains why the OAU stand has been so weakened – for the Organ-isation of African Unity is just like the UN, a reflection of what its members make of it – and why, in particular, so many former French colonies have so easily fallen under the pressure of Paris* and have sunk to the depths of accept-ing, with various nuances, the 'dialogue' with South Africa.

In 1971, matters looked so bad for the OAU that it was thought that its June Summit session would turn into a victory for those African leaders who listen more to Paris and London, but this did not happen and the OAU man-aged to shake off its lethargy; the Western manoeuvre to start the OAU along the treacherous path of 'dialogue' was adroitly exposed by the Nigerian delegate who acted in a manner which would oblige those who wanted to com-promise with South Africa to come out publicly. And this they could never do, because 'dialogue' to start with, is un-acceptable to their own public opinions. A significant anti-colonial victory was scored when the OAU decided to with-draw recognition of the Angolan puppet liberation move-ment of Roberto Holden known as the *Gouvernement Révolutionnaire de l'Angola en Exil* (GRAE), supported by Mobutu's Congo, Tunisia and a few others – but above all by the CIA.

The 9th Summit of the OAU, in June 1972, in Rabat, took place when there was a growing feeling among Heads of State that time had come – at last – to intensify the struggle against white minority regimes, with Portugal becoming the main target. Member countries decided – with the sole exception of Banda's Malawi, which boycotted the Summit – to increase their contribution to the African Liberation Committee by 50 per cent and for the first time Liberation Movements were admitted to the debates with the right to decide on resolutions affecting them; announcing this to the press, the OAU's militant Assistant Secretary, General Mohamed Sahnoun, of Algeria, bluntly said: 'a gross error of the past has thus been corrected, for hitherto Liberation Movements were learning of decisions affecting them sometime after you gentlemen of the press'.

Two other events took place in Rabat concerning the anti-colonial struggle which I feel should be registered in this chapter. It could be said that, for all practical purposes, the CONCP – the Conference of Nationalist Organisations of the Portuguese Colonies – (see the forthcoming chapter, 'The Armed Struggle') had come to an end in this very city of Rabat where it had been created over a decade ago. It could be said that the CONCP was the victim of the realities of geo-politics which cause many to err when speaking of the 'three Portuguese colonies' forgetting that two of them, so different in size and potential – Angola and Mozambique – are located in Southern Africa while tiny Guinea Bissao is located in the much easier context of West Africa. As years went on and each movement got more involved in its own territory, the realities of geo-politics were bound to reveal themselves and the CONCP to become more and more of a theoretical organisation. This tendency increased, with the PAIGC – closer to Algeria and Western and Eastern Europe – inevitably acting more and more as a *cavalier seul*. In 1972 there were growing rumours that Portugal – pressed by London and Washington – would be ready to grant independence to Guinea Bissao – but minus the all-important Cape Verde islands, and the UN decided to recognise the PAIGC as the sole representative of Guinea Bissao. Superficially at least, it looked as if independence might not be that far away for the PAIGC – while in the deep South of Africa both MPLA and FRELIMO were heading for bitter fights with the brutal forces of South Africa. When Amilcar Cabral, a resolute revolutionary, addressed the Heads of State at Rabat, his speech already had the overtones ... of a Head of State.

The second event – one which could have far-reaching consequences in Southern Africa and bring the war to the doors of Luanda – was the 'reconciliation', under OAU auspices, between MPLA and ALNA, the 'Angolan National Liberation Army' – the military arm of the FLNA.

Nothing could better illustrate the importance of this 'reconciliation' – if it works – than the fact that under Roberto Holden, ALNA's only job is, assisted by Mobutu's army, to prevent the MPLA from penetrating Angola from the North, from Zaïre where ALNA is stationed, to re-activate its 1st region which reaches close to Luanda and which has remained isolated for a long time. The 'reconciliation' should in theory at least, for it presupposes that Mobutu would in the final analysis stop preventing the MPLA from crossing his territory, change the face of the war in Angola overnight.

On 30 March 1972 MPLA's 'Fighting Angola' radio (operating from Brazzaville) broadcast the following statement by Agostinho Neto: 'We are in a position to guarantee to all the African countries, whose territories may be used as bases for our national liberation struggle, full respect for their sovereignty ... We guarantee not to interfere in their internal affairs ...' Neto was also to add that the unity of the entire Angolan people was necessary if Angola was to obtain independence.

This broadcast was made with the reconciliation-to-come in view, and to reassure General Mobutu that the MPLA

would not interfere in his domestic affairs, for not only are
there some 600,000 discontented Angolan refugees in and
around Kinshasa, but General Mobutu's reactionary policies
are meeting with opposition within Zaïre itself. The statement also reflected the MPLA's anti-tribal attitude (the
ALNA is entirely tribal) and the priority it gives to unity.
Finally being able to cross Zaïre's border has a political
price which the MPLA was ready to pay.

At Rabat, during a closed session of the OAU, Agostinho
Neto said: 'I am ready for unity [with ALNA] right now
if possible.' Mobutu and Holden looked cornered for in
their minds 'reconciliation' was only a tactic. The Heads of
State asked for reconciliation to be effective as from the
OAU's next summit, with Presidents Gowon of Nigeria and
Boumedienne of Algeria pressurising Mobutu, who was
forced to appear at least as being in favour of reconciliation.
Roberto Holden had for a long time ceased to be a force to
reckon with; many of his followers had already joined
MPLA ranks in Congo-Brazzaville well before the Rabat
meeting. This, Mobutu knew only too well. It is an open
secret that since 1963, under the late Kasavubu, an agreement has existed between Kinshasa and the Portuguese
authorities of Angola under the pretext of 'controlling
communists' and also for continued trade. This accord
was further fortified when in 1969 a state secretary of the
Mobutu government visited the Portuguese. Then too,
Zaïre is, together with Ethiopia, a main concern of the US
Strategic Command in Africa and one hardly sees the
NATO – or the CIA – allowing Mobutu to open wide his
borders to the MPLA.* Real hope lies in the fact that
through this 'reconciliation' the MPLA may be able to
infiltrate some men and equipment to its 1st Region.

The Rabat OAU Summit was described by Colin Legum,
in *The Observer* of 18 June, as the one where African
States appeared more closely united than at any time in the
nine years since the establishment of the Organisation of
African Unity. But this unity was mainly in appearance,

as the OAU could only be a conglomeration of mostly bourgeois African leaders, nominally independent but otherwise still deep in the shadow of colonialism. Freedom fighters at Rabat agreed more with Professor Leonard Barnes* that 'the OAU is nothing more than the continent-wide trade-union of the kleptocrats ... and the mere thought of a pervasive and popular underground movement sends shivers down every kleptocrat's spine'.

The African scenery can be fertile and before the Heads of State met again in the May of 1973, in Addis – to realise among other things that King Hassan of Morocco had still not made good the $1,000,000 contribution to Liberation Movements he had announced with such fanfare at the previous Rabat summit – two unforeseen capital events were to take place. The first – which made world headlines at once – was the assassination of Amilcar Cabral. The second – a closed secret for some time and still not well-known as these lines are being written – was an attempt to liquidate the leader of the MPLA and interrupt the 'Neto trail' which from Zambia's eastern border (it starts in fact, at the port of Dar es Salaam) goes deep into Angola.

The real depth of the 'Neto trail' – almost 3,000 kms long – into the heart of Angola is something the MPLA is religiously silent about. Observers were however surprised to see from a Portuguese military map how unsuspectedly deep this trail had gone into Angola, in the Bie province particularly. The map, dated 'February 1972' and belonging to the 2nd REP Portuguese unit based in Luanda was brought to Amsterdam by a Portuguese officer who deserted. Owing to lack of space it could not be published in this book, but it was reproduced in the Dutch weekly *Vrij Nederland* of 18 August 1973.

On 18 October 1972, addressing a UN Committee in New York, Amilcar Cabral announced that liberated areas of Guinea Bissao would be declared an 'independent state' end of 1972 or beginning 1973. Elections by universal, direct, and secret vote, for a People's National Assembly of Guinea Bissao were already held in April–June 1972. But on 20 January 1973, Cabral was treacherously murdered in front of his own house with two pistol shots, and when he fell, still alive, was finished off with several sprays of automatic weapons. Radio Conakry – as erratic as ever – confused the issue by attributing the murder to 'imperialism and neo-colonialism' when it should in fact have been attributed to the hirelings of imperialism and neo-colonialism. All, including an editorial in the *Times* of London, easily saw in this murder 'the long arm' of Portugal. It remained nevertheless for the facts to be squarely faced – that the very essence of Cabral's murder (perpetrated by at least thirty PAIGC members including the Navy Chief, who was obviously able to penetrate the tight security system surrounding Cabral's house) was a concoction of personal ambitions and tribalism: Guinea Bissao versus the Cape Verde intellectuals, of whom Cabral was the best example. It will obviously not be easy to know in detail the many factors which must have caused Cabral's assassination. For sure, Lisbon cannot have been pleased at the idea of an independent Guinea Bissao. On the other hand such an independent state in the liberated parts of the mainland but under the leadership of a Cape Verdian may have sparked off dormant tribalism among the mainland people, and was ably exploited by the Portuguese. Another obscure point: what role, if any, in Cabral's murder did the dissidents of Sekou Toure play? In November 1970 they had constituted the main force in the Portuguese-led attempts at invading Conakry – was it not Cabral, and not Sekou Toure, who was instrumental in repelling these Portuguese/Sekou Toure dissidents? And had not the Portuguese on this very occasion tried to eliminate Cabral or capture him, by using these dissidents?

An easier explanation could ascribe the whole murder episode to the Portuguese and it may not be irrelevant to remember in this connection a thought of Cabral himself:

'Imperialism is criminal and without scruple ... but we must not put everything on its back, for, as goes an African proverb, rice cooks only inside the cauldron.'
(*Afrique-Asie*, 21 August 1972)

It should also be noted that Cabral's assassination came at a moment when the guerillas had obtained better arms, 122 mm. rockets and ground-to-air missiles, which had put an end to the hitherto unchallenged Portuguese air superiority. In April 1973 the Portuguese Air Commander in Guinea Bissao, Lt.-Col. Almeida Brito himself had been shot down in his Fiat G-91. By 10 September 1973, PAIGC had downed twenty-one planes.

Cabral's untimely death is a severe setback, but there are strong reasons to believe that the very spirit he created will ensure that the fight for liberation of Guinea Bissao and Cape Verde will succeed. Paths of revolution are such that Cabral is neither the first nor the last leader to have been betrayed by the very ones he wanted to free.

Cabral's post of Secretary-General of the PAIGC went to Aristide Maria Pereira, a radio technician aged forty-nine, and a founder member of the PAIGC together with Amilcar Cabral.

Commenting on Cabral's assassination, *The Economist*, of 27 January 1973, said: 'Mr Cabral's achievement was to make the PAIGC into a force which fought with schools, clinics and ballot boxes as well as with weapons, and which can sustain its momentum even without his leadership.'

It was not a prophecy in vain, for Cabral's decision to create an independent Republic of Guinea Bissao – in the liberated areas of Boe, in Eastern Guinea – became a reality on 24 September 1973. Thus came to an end, at least in part, a colony founded by the Portuguese in 1879. Guinea, Togo, Tanzania, Ghana, Nigeria, Mauritania, Congo, Liberia, Algeria, Syria and Yugoslavia – followed by China – at once recognised the new state; more recognition was to come. By 1 October the USSR had become the 44th

nation to recognise the new state. Lisbon branded the pro-
clamation of the republic as an 'act of propaganda ...
which does not correspond at all to conditions reigning in
this Portuguese province'. But in the same breath, Lisbon
announced the election of two deputies to represent in
the National Assembly in Lisbon ... the 'Portuguese State
of India' – Goa, Damao and Diu and the small enclaves of
Dadra and Nagar-Aveli, all lost to invading Indian troops
in 1961!

Luiz Cabral, Amilcar's half-brother, was appointed
President of the Council of State, also remaining Assistant
Secretary-General of the party.

The event also meant the end of a Guinean career for
another of those generals who felt so assured of their
supremacy: General Spinola was replaced as C.-in-C.
Guinea Bissao by General Bettencourt Rodriguez, who had
Angolan experience.

The attempt to eliminate Neto and cut the MPLA's
Zambian link is a curious one. (The noted Italian journalist
Pietro Petrucci was the first to publish an account of this
story in *Afrique-Asie* of 20 August 1973. The very first indication that an attempt against the life of Dr Agostinho Neto
had been discovered and that he was being pressurised
to negotiate with the Portuguese appeared, however, in the
Paris daily *La Croix*, of 18 April 1973.) It can best be told
by going back to 13 December 1972 when the surprising
announcement came from Kinshasa that an MPLA/
FLNA Agreement had been reached under the auspices of
General Mobutu and the Foreign Ministers of Tanzania,
Congo and Zambia. A Supreme Revolutionary Council
for Angola, to be presided over by FLNA with an MPLA
vice-president, was formed with two branches – political,
presided over by FNLA, and military, presided over by
MPLA. Many an observer – left-wing groups in the West
in particular – felt surprised, for had not Roberto Holden
been felt to be a 'racialist' and 'an American agent'? For
the MPLA rank and file – except for faraway units which

could not be reached quickly – there was little surprise, for it was Neto's twenty-third attempt to achieve unity with FLNA 'to avoid fractionalism for if ethnic differences are exploited they can explode into tribal contradictions'. What left-wing theoreticians could not realise were the realities of tribal structures in Angola. Neto has often chosen to spend more time trying to smooth out the differences in the interior – arising from complaints that someone from one tribe had said he had been given less salt or a smaller cake of soap than someone else from a different tribe – than attending a conference abroad. Another point which many others missed is the difference that should be made between Roberto Holden on the one hand and the FLNA militants on the other – of whom an increasing number had been deserting to MPLA camps in the Congo or revolting against Holden. Mobutu troops had to intervene on 26 March 1972 to quash a revolt of FLNA militants against Holden at the Kikunzu base, in the Katanga. Last but not least, there was, and remains, for MPLA the short route from Zaïre, to relieve militants north of Luanda in the 1st Region. These MPLA guerillas have largely been isolated – and squeezed by the Portuguese from the south, and the Holden men from the north – since 1963 when Zaïre (then Congo-Leopoldville) put a forcible end to MPLA presence in its territory.

There was rejoicing among the some 600,000 Angolan refugees in and around the Zaïre capital when for the first time since 1963 an MPLA delegation led by Neto crossed the river from Brazzaville into Kinshasa in December 1972. Neto was preceded and followed on the same voyage by the Ambassadors of China and North Korea with whom General Mobutu, who was at that time playing at being the 'progressive', had established diplomatic relations.

Holden's true feelings about the 'reconciliation' were registered in *The Times* of 27 December 1972 in an interview obviously granted shortly before the Agreement was reached; he stated he was opposed to joining ranks with the 'Communist MPLA'. It was again quite obvious that it was his big boss, General Mobutu, who made him in a short time tactically change his mind. Unfortunately for Holden, his interview was published some two weeks after he had 'agreed to unite with MPLA'.

But very soon it was clear that Mobutu was not genuine in his promise that MPLA would henceforth be allowed to operate from Zaïre. For, it can be disclosed, the very minute the agreement was signed by the FLNA, Neto asked that a small group of MPLA guerillas should come from the Congo 'without weapons' (to satisfy Mobutu), in order to cross Zaïre into Angola from where they would then return with several hundred Angolans. Then, as per the agreement, Holden was to contribute an equal number of men and they would all be trained together by MPLA at one of the many military bases Mobutu had contracted would be put at their disposal. Neto's (test) request has yet to be answered to this date.

What happened next is that during discussions for the 'implementation of the agreement' early in 1973 MPLA and FLNA, who had ironed out most difficulties thanks to the MPLA delegation making all possible concessions, ran into a stumbling-block: Holden insisted that the aim of unification was that of 'obtaining a negotiated peace' with Portugal. Neto stuck to the known MPLA stand – which had been further agreed to by Mobutu himself on 13 December 1972 – that 'liberation will come only after a prolonged struggle', and for the first time broke up the talks, saying he would resume them after General Mobutu, then in Belgium, returned to Kinshasa.

Mobutu, quite an expert in *volte-faces*, stood by Holden's 'negotiated peace' formula and arrested forty MPLA militants in Kinshasa and Matadi accusing them of 'subversive activities'. MPLA negotiators were arrested by FLNA police and others were barred from entering Zaïre. However, 20,000 Portuguese settlers in Zaïre could go about their daily activities in full tranquillity although, as is well known, they constitute a remarkable network of informers and agents for Lisbon particularly in the corrupt climate of Kinshasa.

Mobutu informed Kaunda and Nyerere that he was sticking to his promise to grant 'all facilities' to the MPLA in Zaïre, but that Neto by refusing to cooperate with FLNA was preventing this!

When all this was taking place, Neto was already in possession of two important messages: one, from a friendly power (which cannot be identified) informing him of a plot to 'kill' him; the other from a well-known international organisation (which cannot be disclosed either except to state that it is based in Western Europe) to tell him that Lisbon wanted to contact him for the purpose of finding a solution for a 'negotiated peace'.

The first-mentioned conspirators – one of whom was to toss a hand-grenade at Neto – were discovered in Western Zambia (the former Barotseland) and four of them were executed after a public trial. Daniel Chipenda, a leading member of the 40-man MPLA Executive Committee, turned out to be the leader of the local conspirators, then sought refuge with the Zambian police. Guerillas under his command had already started making trouble by refusing to obey orders on the grounds they they were issued by men 'from another tribe'. Zambian police – still very much under the influence of traditional British training – tried to enter an MPLA camp to free the captive conspirators, but did not succeed. Somewhere else, other members of the Zambian élite class (opposed to Kaunda), which in the past had favoured a tiny Angolan splinter group known as UNITA, started creating problems along the MPLA's supply route from Dar es Salaam and in the border regions.

A noted absentee from the Algiers September Non-Aligned Conference was Dr Agostinho Neto – a man of infinite kindness and resolution, patience and energy; he was at that time the vigilant sentinel of his poems watching over the trail of freedom into the Angola he had started building with literally bare hands, some ten years ago. But, to quote Professor Leonard Barnes once again, 'kleptocrats' see differently and they stand for counter-revolution.

This author learned – the information was quite unknown when this book was going to press and it would certainly create a stir – that General Mobutu had agreed that oil found off Zaïre at Moko IX, and at Mibale IX should be brought by sea and pipe-line through the Portuguese-occupied territory of Cabinda to the Gulf Oil Company terminals in this enclave.

The whole deal was part of a 'second Kuwait' which Gulf Oil had discovered off Cabinda keeping silent about it for obvious political reasons. It was partly with this new find in mind that President Nixon had, in the first half of September, met the Arab threat of oil boycott (subsequently to be implemented) with more self-assurance, saying that the US would nevertheless be able to satisfy its oil requirements. The pressure against Neto to agree to a 'negotiated peace' with Portugal and upon his refusal, the attempt to kill him and with him the MPLA, should now be clearer.

PART II
by ARSLAN HUMBARACI
and NICOLE MUCHNIK

ONE

The History of Portuguese Colonisation in Africa

The Setting

THE empire which Portugal maintains in Africa is two-thirds the size of Europe. Angola, the islands of São Tomé and Príncipe, Guinea Bissao, the Cape Verde Islands and Mozambique together form an area of some 2,057,947 square kilometres. Total population only numbers about 13,500,000, nearly 700,000 of which are Europeans. Portugal herself has an area of 91,900 square kilometres, and a population of 8,600,000 in 1971.

The largest of these provinces is Angola which, with the enclave of Cabinda, is larger than Italy, France and the two Germanies put together. The country is bounded by a low-lying, regular shoreline to the west, the Congo-Kinshasa republic to the north, Zambia to the east and Namibia (formerly South-West Africa) to the south.

The population consists largely of black Bantus. The whites are mostly Portuguese, but there is a large colony of German settlers – the majority with a solid Nazi background – and Italians as well. Small, mostly nomadic, groups of Khoi-San (Boshimas and Hottentots) are to be found in the south and south-east of the country. The Bantus all speak closely related languages and generally have animism as their religion; only a minority have been converted to christianity. The *mestizos*, who are entitled to Portuguese nationality, are considered to be Catholics and are said to number around 25,000.

The capital of Angola is Luanda. Founded in 1575, it is the oldest European settlement south of the equator. Two other large towns are Huambo (Nova Lisboa) and Lobito. The urban population represents 15 per cent of the total population of the country. More than 90 per cent of the Europeans live in the towns.

The Angolan economy is based on the widespread cultivation of equatorial and tropical crops such as tobacco, cotton and coffee – which leaves little room for traditional food crops – and on the exploitation of the country's vast mineral resources. The livestock, such as it is, belongs mostly to the Africans.

Up to 1968, the most important export was coffee, closely followed by diamonds and sisal. Then came iron ore, which has since become the chief export, and oil. Coffee beans alone account for nearly 50 per cent of the total volume of Angolan exports. A tenth of this production goes directly to Portugal; 50 per cent is sent to the United States. Diamonds are mainly exploited by a monopoly known as the Angola Diamond Company (Diamang). The rough diamonds are all exported to the metropolis, where they are merely resold in the same state.

Angola exports nearly 40 per cent of its produce to Portugal, and imports the same percentage. There are strict regulations preventing the colonies from developing manufacturing industries (such as textiles) which could offer competition to those of the metropolis. Thus, Angola imports five times more Portuguese wine each year than it does tractors.

The smallest of the three countries – so-called Portuguese Guinea – is bounded by Senegal in the north and Guinea in the east and south, and includes a belt of off-shore islands (Pecixe, Bissao, Bolama, Como) and the Bijagós archipelago. The Cape Verde Islands, off the coast of Senegal, are also part of this country which is known as Guinea Bissao to anti-colonialists.

There are twenty or so different ethnic groups, which share almost equally the two main religious groupings – Islam and African. At the 1950 census, the main groups were: Balantas, including Balantas Mané and Cunantes or Mansoancas (160,296); Fulas, all groups (108,402); Manjacos (71,712); Mandingas (63,750); Papéis (36,341); Brames or Mancanhas (16,300); Beafadas (11,581); Bijagós (10,332); others (22,743). The Fulahs and the Mandingas follow Islam. The animists are part of an ethnic grouping which extends from Senegal to the Ivory Coast; they have no written language.

Most of the inhabitants live by agriculture. The economy is entirely subservient to the demands of Portugal and since Guinea offers no economic potentialities – with the exception of off-shore oil possibilities – it has been greatly neglected and remains a very poor country, the Cape Verde islands being richer and more developed. This explains, among others, the scarcity of economic statistics on Guinea Bissao.

In peace time, 60 per cent of Guinea Bissao's foreign revenue comes from the cultivation of ground-nuts, imposed on the country by the Portuguese and covering an area of 105,000 hectares; 70 per cent of the production is exported. Next in importance come palm oil and palm nuts, and then rice, which is by far the most profitable crop and also provides food for local consumption. Since the outbreak of the struggle for independence, cultivation of this particular crop has increased substantially in the liberated zones. It should be noted that only 40 per cent of the cultivable land was in use just before the insurrection.

The Guinean economy is in the hands of a powerful Portuguese monopoly, the *Companhia União Fabril* (CUF), which controls all foreign trade and the country's balance of payments in such a way as to provide Portugal with the cheapest possible raw materials in exchange for manufactured goods. The CUF's interests in Guinea dominate the country to such an extent that the repressive measures taken by Portuguese troops were referred to as 'the Company's war' or 'the war of the CUF'. The CUF is a giant company, with further interests in Angolan textiles and Mozambique plantations, and the only Portuguese company to figure among the two hundred largest business concerns outside the USA.

The Antonio Silva Gouveia enterprise (representing CUF) has the monopoly over trade and works as agent for, among others, Ford, Raleigh Industries, and various Portuguese companies. It has invested tens of thousands of contos. It is the largest investor and is followed by Sociedade Commercial Ultramarina, which has invested about 20,000 contos, mainly in grinding of rice and manioc and extraction of vegetable oils. Its liaisons include BP, Goodyear, Dodge, Mercedes-Benz, Citroën, Philips, SKF, Siemens, Singer. Companhia Lusitania de Aluminia da Guiné et de Angola was established by the government of Portugal and a Dutch company (N.V. Biliton Maatshappij) for extracting bauxite. Its capital is 5,000 contos. Esso Exploration Guiné, Inc., has invested 43,500 contos. Unilever is also there.

Coastal minorities such as the Papéis and Manjakos produce good sailors and tend to emigrate to wherever the birth of industry can provide them with employment. There are three main religions; 64 per cent of the population are animists, 35 per cent muslims, and less than 1 per cent christians.

The Guinean population is still 99 per cent illiterate.

The administrative capital is Bissao, a small town of 26,000 inhabitants. The other main centres of population are small ethnic capitals – Kancuru, the chief town of the Manjak-Boks, and Bula, a large Mancagne village. The Bijagós archipelago has remained isolated from the mainland.

The Cape Verde Islands, of which there are ten, grouped off the coast of Senegal, were for a long time used as a staging-point in the slave trade to the Americas. The population was therefore largely intermixed, consisting of the descendants of convicts, sailors, slave traders and slaves. To-day, this coloured population has increased and lives by agriculture – maize, sugar cane, coffee, bananas – and fishing.

For a time it was Portugal's ambition to join Angola to Mozambique and thus gain an empire stretching right across equatorial Africa. But this project was dropped at the time of the Berlin Conference (1885) in the face of the colonial ambitions of France, England, Belgium and Germany, who were in a stronger position than Portugal.

Mozambique lies south of Tanzania, and is bordered by Malawi and Lake Nyasa, Zambia, Rhodesia, South Africa and Swaziland. To the east, it gives on to the Indian Ocean. The country is crossed by numerous rivers, the most important being the Limpopo and the Zambezi.

Although it is smaller than Angola it nevertheless has a larger population, the majority of which are black Bantus. Only half of the foreigners are Portuguese; the other half includes Indians, holders of British passports, and around 30,000 *mestizos*. About 5 per cent of the population are Christian, and there are a few Muslims among the Indians, while the animist Africans form the vast majority. Lourenço Marques, the administrative capital, and Beira, are two important ports.

Mozambique is the fifth largest African producer of sugar (219,000 tons in 1968), sixth among the tea exporting countries (14,251 tons in 1968), and the world's twenty-seventh producer of cotton lint (38,887 tons in 1968). Unshelled cashew production amounted to 132,146 tons in 1968.

Mozambique's next foreign exchange earning sector is transport and communications – rail and roads going from the ports of Beira, Lourenço Marques and Nacala to inland destinations in South Africa, Rhodesia, Malawi and Zambia.

In mining, still at an early stage, Mozambique produced in 1968 – all for export – 3,274·6 tons of bauxite (imported by Rhodesia); 314,408 tons of coal (of which 68,213 tons were imported by Malawi, Kenya and Angola, and the rest consumed locally); beryl, 95·3 tons; bismuthite, 2·1 tons; columbo-tantalite, 62·0 tons; microlite, 90·4 tons (all exported to the USA and the UK). Mozambique also produces 2,655·7 tons of bentonite for export to various countries.

As in the case of Angola, manufacturing industries are few and agro-industrial products like cotton, are obligatorily exported to Portugal as raw material to return to Mozambique as textiles.

In contrast to Angola, the last decade has seen no structural changes in Mozambique's main resources, agriculture remaining the mainstay of the country's economy. It is only lately that mining has become a new venture – a promising one at that.

The six most important agro-industrial exports of Mozambique are cotton, cashews, sisal, copra, sugar and tea. Agriculture contributes about 25 per cent of the GNP and is the principal source of foreign exchange. Mozambique's economically active population is put at 2·6 million, 69 per cent of whom are engaged in agriculture. Still another difference from Angola where European farmers produce the principal share of agricultural exports, is that in Mozambique Africans are active in cotton, cashew and copra production.

The consequences of this kind of economic policy were unequivocally denounced by the Bishop of Beira in 1950:

Whoever has frequent contact with certain of the cotton zones has no difficulty in recognising that the principal effort of the native ... is absorbed by the cotton, and that there remains not much time or effort to grow food which is needed by him and others. I know a region which used to be a granary for lands afflicted with hunger. After the cotton campaign was begun there, the fertile fields ceased to supply food for the neighbouring

populations and the people of the region itself also began
to feel hunger. There belongs to my diocese a region in
which for six months the black spectre of hunger reaped
the lives of the inhabitants.*

The late FRELIMO President Eduardo Mondlane,
quoted* a Zambezian peasant engaged in compulsory tea-
cultivation as saying: 'We were forced to work on tea but
we didn't know what it tasted like – we couldn't afford it.'

The Portuguese colonies in Africa are completed by the
islands of São Tomé and Príncipe, some 300 kms. off the
West African coast, also comprising a group of isles:
Cabras, Santana, Quixiba and the Sete Pedras, Rolas,
Gabado and Coco. The Seven Stones (Sete Pedras) are really
fourteen isles.

This 'overseas province' was famous for slave trading and
sugar-cane cultivation – it served for a long time, as a safe
transit port for slave-traders away from the dangers of the
coast. A Portuguese decree dating from the sixteenth
century stipulated that 'each colonist take one woman and
give her children'. The English, Dutch and French, who
needed slave labour for their own sugar-cane plantations,
tried several times to conquer São Tomé and Príncipe. Denmark, West Germany, the Netherlands and South Africa
are today the main buyers of the islands' coffee, copra, coco-
nuts and cocoa.

Nowadays, cheaper labour is imported from Angola,
Mozambique and Cape Verde.

São Tomé and Príncipe are very much the domains of
Portugal's richest families known as the 'great families'
who are major stockholders of the *Banco Nacional Ultramarino* (BNU).

This bank, one of the oldest in the world, has as associates the Crédit Franco-Portugais, le Comptoir National
d'Escompte de Paris, the Midland Bank Executor and
Trust Company, the Westminster Bank Ltd, and the
Spanish-American Bank.

A CONCP bulletin dating from 1968 listed as follows the 'great families':

Sommer (great agricultural family allied with the Mello family in CUF); Teotonio Pereira (former ambassador to London and Minister of the Presidency); Cohen; De Brée (Alvaro de Brée is one of the administrators of Diamang – Angola Diamond Company); Stau Monteiro; Holstein Beek (Duke of Pamela); Pinto Basto; Soares de Albergaria; Monteiro Belard; Sousa Lara (director of CADA of Angola). And certain financiers such as D. Diogo Pessanha, Antonio Piano, and D. Arthur Menezes Correia de Sa (Viscount of Merceana), Vice-Governor of BNU.

According to Portuguese colonial theories, São Tomé and Príncipe are not part of Africa, therefore the *autoctón* are not *mestiços* but *civilizados*.

São Tomé is a strategic stopover for military aeroplanes and also for civilian airlines which have to avoid the African continent.

The 1969 air-lift relief operations to Biafra (some forty take-offs and landings a day) created a boom on the island.* But this was not to last long and in February 1970, when the Nigerian civil war came to an end, it also cut huge profits for São Tomé and the governor of the islands rushed to Lisbon to seek economic assistance.

While it is clear that nationalist activities in these islands will have to wait for MPLA to establish itself on the coast of Angola – or incitements may come from Nigeria – by 1968 the Portuguese had already drastically increased their military presence from a few dozens to 3,000 men.

Nationalist agitation on the islands dates back to 1530 when a black slave named Amador managed to stage a revolt, liberate part of São Tomé and proclaim himself king for nearly a year. More recently political consciousness started taking shape in 1947 when intellectuals, and the youth in particular, became more active – on 1 February

1953 the first anti-Portuguese pamphlets appeared. Troubles followed in the plantations and over 1,000 natives were killed. On 11 September 1965 a nationalist movement was formed, the CLSTP – *São Tomé and Príncipe Liberation Committee*. In August 1963 a twenty-four hour strike brought 90 per cent of the islands' agricultural workers to a standstill. Since then political deportation, imprisonment, censorship and corporal punishment – lashing – have been in full swing.

Portugal – The First to Come, The Last to Go

The history of Portuguese colonialism in Africa stretches from 1445 right up to the present day, and it is in many ways a classic example of its kind. The Portuguese were the first to approach the unexplored continent, by way of the Cape Verde Islands. In the fifteenth century, Portugal was at the height of her power, and at the instigation of Henry the Navigator she began a systematic exploration of the African continent. The original aim was merely to establish trading posts on the route to the Indies. Africa was no more than an obligatory staging-point on this route. But with the beginnings of the slave trade in the sixteenth century, the trading posts, and Africa itself, became of major importance.

Originally undertaken for purely commercial reasons, the Portuguese conquest of Africa was to become a classic case of colonialist occupation. Today its territories are being subjected to economic exploitation by international forces – for American, French, German, English and, above all, South African interests are taking over in the face of Portugal's inability to exploit her own colonies.

After the discovery of the Cape Verde Islands, Portuguese ships reached the Gulf of Guinea in 1449, then the islands of São Tomé and Príncipe in 1471. In 1482, Diego Cão reached the mouth of the Congo, in what is now Angola. In 1490, Vasco da Gama rounded the Cape of Good

Hope and founded a trading post on the eastern seaboard of Africa – Quelimane in Mozambique. In forty-five years, Portugal had marked out her claim in Africa – this was nearly five centuries ago. The Portuguese had been the first to arrive, and they would be the last to go.

But the interior of the continent was still unexplored, and the Cape Verde Islands and São Tomé were uninhabited. At first sight they seemed to have little to offer and so the Portuguese were slow to occupy them. A few posts were set up, however, and the equatorial vegetation of São Tomé and Príncipe prompted the idea of cultivating sugar cane and collecting valuable resins from the forest. The islands were then settled with Jews, convicts deported from Europe, and Africans from the mainland.

On the continent itself, the trading posts multiplied, complete with ports and military garrisons. In Guinea, the Portuguese traders, known as *lançados*, dealt with small ethnic groups of fishermen and rice-growers without any centralised power. In 1690, an embryo administration was established with the 'grand captaincy' of Cacheu, complemented in 1692 by the 'grand captaincy' of Bissao. It was not until after the Treaty of Berlin in 1885 that the Portuguese attempted to conquer the interior of the country.

In Angola, the Portuguese came into conflict with the powerful kingdom of the Kongo. For four centuries, the Angolans were to rise intermittently in different places, in opposition to the Portuguese occupation and military conquest. A working relationship was nevertheless established between the two thrones, and for a long time the court of the kingdom of the Kongo benefited from the attentions of Portuguese teachers and priests in exchange for tolerating the commercial activities of the *lançados*.

We may wonder if the powerful King of the Kongo obeyed the same laws as the Ashanti chiefs, who were given the following warning whenever they received their peoples:

Tell him that
We do not wish for greediness
We do not wish that he should curse us
We do not wish that his ears should be hard of hearing
We do not wish that he should call people fools
We do not wish that he should act on his own initiative
We do not wish things done as in Kumasi
We do not wish that it should ever be said
'I have no time. I have no time.'
We do not wish personal abuse
We do not wish personal violence.*

Ten million slaves

Since the American Indians displayed a distinct reluctance to submit to the white invader and cooperate in his plans for exploiting their natural resources, there was nothing for it but to search for cheap labour elsewhere. Since slavery was an accepted custom in the Mediterranean, the Europeans felt no hesitation in helping themselves to whatever source could be found. The Africans fulfilled the necessary conditions – they were strong and used to a tropical and equatorial climate. In order to ensure a ready supply of them, the Europeans had only to build fortresses alongside the trading posts which would serve as bases both for the slave traders' ships sailing to the Americas and for armed raids into the interior. Thus, in 1576, the fortress of Luanda was built alongside the little consulate of São Paolo in Angola.

Colonial authors have been only too ready to point out that slavery in Africa often found support amongst the Africans themselves. Certain ethnic groups sometimes even acted as procurers for the Europeans. However, there are two features of the situation which must be borne in mind. On the one hand, certain African societies had a genuine class structure, and it was because of this that in some cases the sovereign did not hesitate to hand over his subjects, or those of a dangerous vassal, to the slave traders. On the other hand, since the occupying forces were better armed than they were, the African peoples were faced with a choice between reluctant collaboration or extermination. These colonial authors have also overlooked that in other societies, white in particular, men have not been different, or kinder, in their treatment of each other. At the same time, we cannot ignore the innumerable resistance movements and attempts at national reconstruction which marked the history of slavery in Africa for three centuries. In Angola, for instance, the so-called 'mystical' and 'irredentist' movements were nothing less than desperate attempts at liberation inspired by growing nationalist feelings.

In telling the story of slavery in the Portuguese colonies, we can omit Portuguese Guinea. In fact the Portuguese never really succeeded in occupying the country and were therefore in no position to strip it of its manpower.

Angola was the first region to be subjected to the hordes of slave traders, and for a long time bore the full brunt of their operations. Since it faced the Atlantic, Angola was a more obvious choice than Mozambique for the navigators leaving for the New World. There was a large native population and the Portuguese could count on the cooperation of the ruling classes. Thus it was Angola which paid the heaviest price – in three hundred years four million Angolans were unloaded from the slave ships on to the shores of the Americas. To this number must be added the proportion who were shipwrecked or died during the crossing – in some cases as many as 80 per cent. It is for this reason that Angola has to this day remained a thinly populated country in comparison with the regions of central Africa which were more protected from slavery. There were numerous racialist justifications of slavery, but perhaps the most amazing of all was that of the Liverpool slave merchants who said:

Africans being the most lascivious of human beings,

may it not be imagined that the cries they let forth, at being torn from their wives, proceed from the dread that they will never have the opportunity of indulging their passions in the country to which they are embarking?*

In Mozambique, the slave trade was not established until the beginning of the nineteenth century. Previously, the Portuguese had tried to penetrate into the interior of the country on several occasions, without success, particularly along the Zambezi river in search of the fabulous mineral riches of the Monomotapa. It was not until the beginnings of industrial civilisation, which, contrary to general belief, did not bring about an immediate end to slavery, that the Portuguese managed to tap this vast supply of human resources. Angola had been squeezed dry, and now it was the turn of Mozambique. The first stages of industrial development in North America called for labour, and for thirty years the slave trade provided it. Then the emigrating proletariat of Europe took the place of the slaves, and the practice of slavery itself fell into disfavour in this part of Africa at least. Meanwhile, despite the first anti-slavery laws passed in Portugal in 1834, the slave trade continued, aided considerably by the coming of the steamship. Between 1800 and 1850, 25,000 slaves were exported each year – more than one million in fifty years. The new laws of 1838 and 1878 did little to change this situation, and the French slave traders – who usually acted as intermediaries between the two continents – continued their activities until the demand had dried up completely. It was the first time that decisions emanating from the metropolis had met with opposition from the Portuguese colonists. A similar conflict was experienced later by France and Great Britain in dealing with their own colonies. In Portugal's case it was prevented from increasing by a return to power of the great colonial families in Lisbon.

Occupation becomes necessary

The end of slavery was an important turning point in the history of Portuguese colonialism. Since Portugal's vast territories in Africa could no longer be used for such immediately lucrative ends as the trade in human beings, other resources had to be found, and for this it was necessary to penetrate into the interior of the continent and encourage white immigration – in fact to 'occupy' the colonies.

By now the European powers had carved up the African continent between them. The Berlin Conference had recently marked out the French and English empires in Africa. Portugal was in no position to contest the claims of France, England, Germany and Belgium, all in full industrial development, and found her ambitions severely restricted as a result. The old dream of an equatorial empire reaching in an unbroken line from the Atlantic to the shores of the Indian Ocean faded away in the face of reality. The new states were now carefully demarcated, the frontiers traced out – though this did not prevent England from laying claim to Mozambique shortly afterwards. It was only after arbitration by France and Germany and then the signature of a *modus vivendi* in 1871 that Portugal was able to keep it.

The fact was that since the beginning of the nineteenth century, Portugal had entered on a period of stagnation, and even of regression in some areas. The Portuguese maritime adventure, which had begun so brilliantly, could have led to an accumulation of capital and subsequent industrial growth inside the metropolis. However, nothing of the kind happened, and imperialist Portugal squandered its colonial riches on prestige and consumer goods. When the young industrial powers set out to conquer the world in their turn, Portugal had little to offer in the way of competition; in Africa all she had done was to occupy a few stretches of coast, at home in Europe she was quite the opposite of an industrialising nation.

After the Berlin Conference, Portugal no longer had any choice. If she wished to retain her territories in Africa, she was obliged to take 'effective control' of them, whether she liked it or not; otherwise they would fall into the clutches of the other colonial powers.

The process of occupation was not easy. Everywhere, the Portuguese troops met with armed resistance from the inhabitants. In Guinea:

> This provoked an immediate reaction on the part of the people. First those on the coast: The Manjakos, particularly the Papeis, in the zone that today is made up by the island of Bissao; the Balantas, a little further inland; the Fulahs; the Mandingas – and practically all the peoples of our country resisted the Portuguese occupation, resistance the Portuguese later called the 'wars of pacification', and which lasted for a period of a half-century in which, according to Teixeira de Mota, almost no day went by without a confrontation between our people and the Portuguese.*

Several thousand Manjakos went into voluntary exile after their defeat at the hands of the Portuguese. The Bijagós archipelago, off the Guinean coast, was not effectively subdued until 1936.

In Angola, the history is no less marked by frenzied resistance and vicious battles against the occupying forces. Queen N'Zinga Mbandi is venerated even today for having mobilised her tribes against the invader between 1635 and 1655. King Mandume and many others fought against the Portuguese. The effective occupation of the territory after the 1914-18 war was accompanied by thousands of deaths.

In Mozambique, the resistance was equally long drawn out. There were bloody battles at Magul (September 1895) and Coolela (November 1895). Everywhere the Africans responded to colonisation with spirited counter-attacks, the most important of which was led by General Magigwane, the chief of the Emperor Gungunhana's armies, against the

Portuguese port of Palule. The wars against the invader ceased temporarily in 1920 with the suppression of the Barwe insurrection.

What is the current state of Portuguese emigration to her overseas territories? Today Portugal, more than any other European country, is a land of emigration. Every year, thousands of Portuguese workers have to depart from their country, often leaving their women and children behind them, in order to seek a living for themselves and their dependents elsewhere. They are received willy-nilly by France, England, Germany, Belgium, Switzerland, and the United States, who give them work and exploit them as they may. In the case of France, this exploitation is particularly brazen since there is no formal agreement between the governments concerned and the Portuguese workers who secretly cross the border are completely in the hands of their employers. The authorities are well aware of the situation – but the fact is that it is a valuable source of cheap labour for French industry. Portuguese priests make sure that these modern slaves accept their fate with duly Christian resignation.

Things are different in the case of the 'Portuguese Overseas Territories'. Between 1951 and 1964, while the birth rate increased from 106 in a thousand to 120 in a thousand, the net emigration to foreign countries continued to be three times as great as emigration to the colonies – the figures for 1951 and 1964 respectively being 36·9 and 31·5 per thousand for foreign countries, and 12·1 and 11·2 per thousand for the overseas possessions. Thus in thirteen years Portuguese emigration to the colonies had shown no increase, in spite of the frantic efforts of the country's leaders in Lisbon. It had remained practically stable both in absolute terms and in proportion to the overall figure. Clearly, it was not only the search for work but also a reluctance to go and fight in the African bush which prompted the clandestine movements across the frontiers of Europe.

Today, the lack of Portuguese emigration to the colonies is no doubt explained by the revolts which have taken place in the three countries. The authorities in Lisbon try every possible means of forcing the soldiers who have just finished their military service in the colonial wars to settle in the Overseas Territories. Their attempts meet with ever-decreasing success, since the ex-soldiers have no desire to settle in areas which they know from first-hand experience are not 'pacified', or if they are will not remain so for long. Thus the Angolan government has deplored the fact that only 4,800 soldiers have decided to stay in the country since the beginning of the war. The third Five Year Plan drawn up by the Caetano government for the years 1968-73 notes that the European colonists prefer to settle in industrial areas. One of the reasons behind the mammoth hydro-electric projects in the colonies, such as Cabora Bassa in Mozambique, is that they are supposed, in theory at least, to attract a substantial white colonial population, with local African residents being herded away from these regions for 'security reasons'.

Portuguese colonial theory

Perhaps more than any other country with colonial ambitions, Portugal has tried to justify its system of colonisation by means of ethical arguments. And more than in any other case also, there is a wide gap between the ideological justification and reality.

The main thesis of the Portuguese ruling class is that Portuguese colonisation starts from a different basis than the colonial activities of other countries. While other forms of colonisation, and particularly the Anglo-Saxon form, may be considered as purely commercial operations, the Portuguese effort is, they claim, ethically motivated. Portuguese colonialism, it is maintained, has always favoured the most civilised forms of commercial interchange, accompanied by racial mixing and the exchange of moral and religious values. Together with his trade the Portuguese colonist has always sought to give the African the benefit of his anti-racialist views, his penchant for hard work, his Christian faith and all the values which accompany it. No people in the world could resist the attractions of such a scheme for long, since they are the attractions of truth itself. In fact the Portuguese concept of man is the true model of humanity. A day will come when the African Portuguese and the metropolitan Portuguese will form one single people, for the greater good of mankind.

Many people in Europe accept this theory – since it enables some to square their consciences and others to make vast profits. However, the historical reality of Portuguese colonisation is, in fact, somewhat different. The theory is merely a fabrication designed to uphold the myths cherished by the Portuguese ruling class, and it does not appear particularly original when compared with other, already existing systems of a similar nature.

In his remarkable study of Angola, Professor James Duffy calls 'sheer fantasy' all 'talk of civilizing missions' of Portugal in her colonies.* For example, the claim that Portuguese colonisation was based on ethical motives right from the beginning is precisely what makes it no different from any of the others. All the colonial governments have always taken the precaution of declaring that they were pursuing ethical motives. Yet, neither during the centuries of slavery, nor during the periods of territorial occupation, was there any real difference between the attitude of a Portuguese conqueror and of his Spanish or Dutch counterpart. The only point on which Portuguese attitudes differ radically from those of the other colonial powers is in the 'institution' of forced labour, which has been carried on right up to the present day. This is a piece of ethical originality which Portugal has little reason to be proud of.

The Portuguese also emphasise the multiracial or non-racialist nature of their colonisation. In fact, none of the colonial enterprises were deliberately racialist at the start, and yet they all became so. Colonisation in itself surely implies the respecting of individual and collective rights, otherwise it would be called by another name.

The Portuguese boast of the large number of mixed marriages in their territories, but here again the claim is of little consequence. They only take place among the lower classes and the percentage is no higher than that in South Africa before racism became an official doctrine. In fact, racial mixing is more an indication of a particular type of colonial settlement – with small traders and farmers and retired sailors predominating in place of industrialists, administrators and technicians – rather than of a deliberate ethical standpoint.

Adrian Guelke, in a remarkable study on the myth of Portuguese non-racialism, wrote in the *New Statesman* of 20 July 1973, that with more Portuguese women having emigrated to the Colonies since World War II mixed marriages had diminished and the proportion of mulattoes to the total population in both Angola and Mozambique had declined sharply. A Portuguese anthropologist, Jorge Dias, commented on the fact that mixed unions were increasingly placed beyond the social pale.

Portuguese attitudes towards miscegenation had historically been very equivocal, the myth notwithstanding. In 1944 Vincent Ferreira, a former Colonial Minister and High Commissioner of Angola, described it as a grave error. Adrian Guelke goes on to say:

The origin of the belief that an absence of colour consciousness is a special feature of the Portuguese national character lies in miscegenation. It is summed up in the proverb that 'God made the white men and God made the black men, but mulattoes were made by the Portuguese.' A comparison of the record of British and French colonialisation with that of the Portuguese bears out the truth of this remark. The explanation is simple: the large preponderance of white males over white females in Portugal's colonies during most of her rule.

For example, as late as 1902, the number of white women in the capital of Angola, Luanda, barely reached a hundred. All but eight were the wives of deported criminals. Nor was the inter-marriage that took place in Portuguese Africa by any means unique. The Coloured population in South Africa is a permanent reminder that the pattern of race relations in South Africa was similar in the 19th Century to that in Portugal's colonies in the first half of this.

We shall see later what the Portuguese have achieved in the field of education; but turning to another aspect of cultural assimilation we find the disconcerting fact that even the Portuguese church has not proved particularly eager to convert the natives to Christianity. In Guinea there are less than 1 per cent Christians, and no priests; in Mozambique around 5 per cent Christians. Admittedly, in the north of Mozambique and above all in Guinea, there was considerable competition from Islam, but here there is a paradox: the spread of Christianity in the Portuguese colonies was far less marked than in other African countries where the colonisers appeared less troubled by religious considerations and where Islam was even more strongly entrenched.

Another aspect of the Portuguese colonial system to be considered is the legislation applied in the colonies. There is, it is said, nothing in Portuguese legislation to prevent an African from acceding to the highest office in his native country and even in the metropolis. A 'civilised' Angolan could equally well be an administrator in Angola or in government service in Portugal.

In actual fact, nothing could be further from the truth. In Guinea, for instance, it is only a handful of *assimilados* from the Cape Verde Islands who have succeeded in becoming officials.* The population of Brazil, though almost entirely Portuguese in origin, had to gain its independence before it could govern its own country. As long ago as 1962,

Professor J. Duffy denounced the 'myth of Luso-African solidarity', saying that the Portuguese had tried to turn their 'sentimental association with the one-time Portuguese colony of Brazil into diplomatic advantage' by wanting people to believe that racial harmony really existed in Brazil. This assertion of the American professor was to be confirmed almost ten years later in a story front-paged in *The Times*,* whose headline read: 'Brazil racial harmony is largely a myth.'

In the African colonies native participation in the institutions of the countries has to all intents and purposes never existed. The colonies are and remain 'white men's colonies' and the native who is not a *'cidadão Português originário'* (citizen of Portuguese birth), who speaks *'linguas nativas e atrasadas'* (backward native languages), who has no *'formaçao portuguêsa'* (Portuguese formation), who is a *'preto'* (black) or *'mistiço'* (half-caste), who is part of *'gente bruta que não vive que na mata'* (people who are no more than savages living in the forest), is not, according to Portuguese legislation,* entitled to be considered *'civilizad'*.

At Carmona, Angola, 'a charming woman' of the Portuguese upper class told a French correspondent: *'Mais, Monsieur, un noir parmi les blancs, c'est comme une mouche dans un verre de lait.'*

In fact, only a few individuals have managed to gain a few privileges, but in this respect there is no comparison with the British colonies, and even less with the French. The Portuguese system is much more of a closed shop than the other colonial systems. The following comments, made about Guinea Bissao, give some idea of the reality of Portuguese colonisation:

The Portuguese colonial, including the overseer, always showed – through ignorance many times, through misinformation at other times, through his need to dominate almost always – a great lack of respect, of consideration for the African personality, the African culture. It is enough to see, for example, how Europe (principally France, England and Belgium) filled up with works of African art; it opened the way to the universal knowledge of the abilities of the African; of African culture in general; of their religions, of their philosophic conceptions. In other words, the way in which the African confronts the reality of the world with cosmic reality. In Portugal no such thing occurred. Either because generally the colonial who was sent to our territories was ignorant, or because the intellectuals were never interested, the Portuguese did not know the African even though they came from the European country with the most colonies in Africa.*

TWO

Five Centuries of European Presence – The Profits and Losses

> There was something in this conquest that was even
> more ruinous of existing society than forced labour, fire-
> arms and the rest could ever be by themselves. This new
> factor was the expansive nature of European civilisation.*

IN the final analysis, none of the colonial enterprises can
be described as good. There is no colonial power which can
boast of having fulfilled its 'ideal' and carried out its 'civilising mission'. Colonisation did not construct a new society,
it did not 'civilise' Africa, did not modernise it as it would
have become modernised without foreign influence. Naked
commercialism wiped out the old values and traditions
without putting anything in their place. A multitude of
half-baked structures and systems was erected, only to be
rejected today by the Europeans who invented them.

It is one of the tasks of this book to see what Portugal has
contributed to her colonies and to reckon up, however
briefly, the profits and losses of her achievement.

One per cent of Africans at School

In 1919, at the International Labour Conference in
Geneva, a delegate from the Portuguese government declared:

> The assimilation of the so-called inferior races, by
> cross-breeding, by means of the Christian religion, by the
> mixing of the most widely divergent elements; freedom

of access to the highest offices of state, even in Europe – these are the principles which have always guided Portuguese colonisation in Asia, in Africa, in the Pacific, and previously in America.

We can consider this statement as a declaration of intent and see if, half a century later, the results have matched up to the promises. Salazar himself made a reckoning of sorts in 1964, when he said:

> For Africa, independence was a catastrophe. The leaders fought each other with knives and pistols, while the population were once again reduced to famine, epidemics, and the *lex talionis* of the precolonial era. It is not enough for men to claim the right to freedom, they must also be capable of making proper use of it. And one is forced to observe that in Africa the result has been a total failure, because it was thought that blacks could replace whites everywhere. Now this is not true. Only the whites are capable of planning and organising an activity. One man had understood this, and that was Tshombe. I should not be accused of racialism just because I say that the blacks do not have the same capabilities as the whites. It is a self-evident observation, based on experience. The blacks need to be organised.*

There is therefore little reason to expect that the Portuguese would have either wished, or known how, to educate and train the native organisers needed for the countries' development. Which brings us to the question of what system of education – if indeed there was a system – the Portuguese adopted in their Overseas Territories. Is it like the French system – excessively selective but offering the same curricula as in the metropolis? Or like the English and Belgium systems – with a very broad elementary basis, but differing considerably from that given at home? The French system could be described as 'assimilationist' and the English and Belgian as 'popular', and in theory the

Portuguese system, as laid down, should contain something of each.

In actual fact, on the one hand there is no application of the 'assimilationist' doctrine, and on the other hand the schooling rate is ridiculously low. There are two schooling systems in the colonies. The first is confined to Portuguese children and 'civilised' *mestizos*, and follows the same curricula as are taught in Lisbon. The second, known as 'adaptive education', is given out by the Catholic Church. It consists of four years' schooling only and is officially designated for Africans.

Another surprise is the proportion of the population who actually receive this education. In Guinea, less than 1 per cent of Africans were in African schools in 1960. Throughout the whole colonial period only fourteen Guineans have obtained a certificate of higher education.

In Angola, also in 1960, 60,000 Africans were receiving elementary education, which – bearing in mind the fact that 50 per cent of the population are under twenty – amounts to less than 3 per cent of the total. Less than 500 Africans were receiving elementary vocational training and the only teacher's training college for Africans contained less than 300 pupils. This college enables primary school classes to be started for 2,000 more pupils each year, but unfortunately this is not even enough to match the rise in population.

On the side of the Europeans and assimilated *mestizos*, 25,000 pupils are in school. Considering the total number of Portuguese in Angola, the schooling rate in this sector is higher than that of the metropolis, where nearly 50 per cent of the population are illiterate. Secondary education in grammar schools and technical colleges takes in nearly 8,000 students, the overwhelming majority of whom are metropolitan Portuguese in origin.

The figures for school attendance in Mozambique are of roughly the same order. In Guinea Bissao, there are two establishments on the Cape Verde Islands which are providing a first generation of teachers.

In order to appreciate the full significance of these figures, we must compare them with those supplied by the countries which have recently gained their independence. The ex-Belgian Congo, for instance, inherited a six-year primary education system taking in 1½ million African pupils, which in absolute terms is thirty times more than in Angola, and in proportion to the difference in population between the two countries represents ten times more children in school.

In the ex-British regions of Africa the average figures are almost as high as in the Congo. In countries which were colonised by the French the educational pyramid is generally somewhat narrower at the base. However, even in the most underprivileged countries – Niger and Upper Volta – the schooling rate is still twice that in the Portuguese colonies. The latter have produced practically no African teachers at university level.

One doctor to 18,000 inhabitants

Figures relating to the systems of hygiene in the three countries are hard to obtain. The only country about which we have relatively precise information is Angola. Here the frightening fact emerges that it was only in 1960 that Portugal took the step of inaugurating a proper medical system, and this consisted of 250 doctors and about 1,000 nurses and medical auxiliaries for the whole country – or one doctor for every 18,000 inhabitants. Most of these doctors reside in the towns and a number of them deal with Europeans only. Eighteen state hospitals and sixty-seven private hospitals or clinics provide a total of around 4,000 beds, or one bed for every 1,200 inhabitants. A direct result of this situation is that the infant mortality rate is the highest in the world. The average life expectancy is around thirty years and the population growth rate is less than 2·3.

To take another example, in 1954, Teixeira da Mota* painted a particularly distressing picture of the situation in

Portuguese Guinea. The great majority of the urban and rural population was suffering from ankylostomiasis, a parasitic disease caused by nematodes or hookworms and producing diarrhoea, anaemia and cardiac weakness. According to the same author the infant mortality rate was 600 in 1,000. Sleeping sickness was endemic in nearly 40 per cent of the villages, as was malaria and various forms of dysentery. Obviously the 'organisation' without which, according to Salazar, the blacks are incapable of doing anything, was sorely lacking in this instance.

The Contratado *and the Worker*

Lacking education and adequate medical care, the African worker fares no better when it comes to the organisation of labour.

Like practically all the colonialists, the Portuguese failed to integrate the working population into a national economy. Thus in Guinea, Angola and Mozambique, there are two separate methods of production, one traditional and the other capitalist. In the case of Portuguese colonisation, the traditional economy is more prevalent than elsewhere. In Guinea it is practically the only one in existence. In Angola, as in Mozambique, the capitalist sector is represented by the big plantations and mining concessions belonging to colonists or mostly to non-Portuguese foreign companies. The fruits of this type of production are destined exclusively for export. For example, 75 per cent of Angolan coffee, the country's chief export which brought in £48 million in 1969, is produced by 550 European plantations and in Mozambique the average land acreage occupied by white settlers is sixty times that of Africans.

It must be said straight away that all the colonising nations made use of forced labour in one form or another to work their mines and estates. But only the free state of the Congo – later the Belgian Congo – the French equatorial territories and the Portuguese colonies used it on a large scale. Moreover the Belgians and the British – and later the

French – fairly quickly realised that there was everything to be gained from allowing their labour force to become consumers of local and imported products. They, therefore, began to pursue what was known as the 'full belly policy' whereby the African work force was left open to the law of supply and demand, and allowed to come and go more or less freely, assisted by a network of medical and domestic facilities. Nothing of the kind happened in the Portuguese colonies. Even today, the Portuguese African worker is recruited by force and separated from his ethnic group and his milieu, often for several years at a time. For millions of small farmers and their families the results of this compulsory labour are disastrous. In the absence of all the adult males, rural life has become considerably impoverished.

In 1935 an official report on Nyasaland – now Malawi – stated:

> The whole fabric of the old order of society is undermined when 30 to 60 per cent of the able-bodied men are absent at one time. Emigration, which destroys the old, offers nothing to take its place, and the family-community is threatened with complete dissolution.*

And according to a report by an Inspector-General of the Portuguese Colonies in 1947, forced labour is 'in some ways worse than simple slavery'.

> Under slavery, after all, the native is bought as an animal: his owner prefers him to remain as fit as a horse or an ox. Yet here [in Angola] the native is not bought – he is hired from the State, although he is called a free man. And his employer cares little if he sickens or dies, once he is working, because when he sickens or dies his employer will simply ask for another.*

Whereas the English established a considerable number of aboriginal tenant farmers in their colonies, the Portuguese make use of *contratados*, as those subjected to forced labour are called. In Angola this type of employment covers more than half of the wage-earning population. The actual wages are paltry and the workers are generally taken far from their homes. The International Labour Organisation Council has investigated this practice and denounced it on several occasions. Compared with that of the *contratados* the lot of the workers in the industrial sector is enviable indeed; in fact they can be considered as ordinary wage-earners – though like their counterparts in Portugal they do not have the right to strike.

A particularly questionable agreement was that passed between Portugal and South Africa in 1928, whereby 100,000 workers from Mozambique are handed over each year to go and work in the South African mines. In return for this South Africa undertook to make use of the ports of Mozambique for 47.5 per cent of its exports, which assures the Lisbon regime of a substantial income in foreign currency. This agreement is still in force and has been ratified several times since 1928. The depopulation of the southern half of Mozambique is entirely due to this form of legalised slavery.

Exploitation by old-fashioned capitalism

Economically speaking, the colonies are above all a protected market for the metropolis. This means both that their production is closely geared to the latter's need in raw materials, and that they are forced to buy the finished products they need from Portugal, being forbidden to manufacture them on the spot so that they do not compete with the metropolitan industries.

While the economy of the Portuguese colonies was for a long time dominated by agriculture, mining activities now play an important part also. The agriculture is of two kinds – one conducted by small farmers who also indulge in trading on a small scale, and the other, consisting of big plantations, which is in the hands of the state or other large enterprises, foreign or Portuguese.

Portugal's economic hold over its colonies involves on the one hand protectionism and on the other the servicing of foreign monopolies – mainly French, Belgian, British, West German, Japanese and South African – by the Portuguese ruling classes.

There are numerous examples of protectionism. In Mozambique and Angola, for instance, products such as cotton which could be converted on the spot have to be sent to the metropolis and then brought back again in their finished form. Angolan cotton production (71,000 tons in 1969) was expected to reach 80,000 tons, worth £6 million as raw material, for Portugal's textile industry. Mozambique, where there are 310,000 hectares under cotton, produced 122,000 tons, almost all of which was forcibly purchased by Lisbon at prices below world average. The story is the same with Mozambique's 300,000 tons of sugar produced in 1970. Angola and Mozambique have to export a high percentage of their production to Portugal and receive the same percentage of imported products back from Lisbon. There are also the restrictions which Lisbon imposes on the few manufacturing industries in the colonies which might compete with the metropolis. Thus the construction of textile manufacturing plants is forbidden in Mozambique.

In fact, Portugal's determination to export her products to the colonies is largely due to the fact that they are all of a particular nature and cannot find an adequate market elsewhere. In 1969, for instance, Portugal's biggest exports, in order of importance, were: products of the cotton industry; cork and articles made of cork; wine; fish preserves; wood, charcoal, resin and tomato juice.* This list shows clearly that the Portuguese economy is in no state to compete with that of the other more highly developed European countries.

The second feature of the economic relations between Portugal and her colonies is equally indicative of the underdeveloped state of the metropolis. Portugal does not have the facilities to cut Angolan diamonds, refine oil or manufacture finished products from iron. In order to gain some profit from these cheaply extracted raw materials, the state acts simply as an agent for them, taking its percentage before passing them on to the powerful economic empires established elsewhere. And the big business families of Lisbon serve as intermediaries in these deals.

The basic function of the colonies is clearly outlined by the Third Quinquennial Plan drawn up by the Lisbon government for 1968-73.

> The metropolis provides a large proportion of the raw materials, foodstuffs, high quality finished articles and manufactured goods. The Overseas Territories and other underdeveloped regions receive a large proportion of the metropolis's industrial exports, in exchange for which they provide basic raw materials and foodstuffs.

The result is an apparently stable economic situation. Angola sells more goods to the metropolis than it buys back, exporting coffee (47 per cent), rough diamonds (16 per cent), maize (15 per cent), sisal (15 per cent), and iron (3 per cent); and importing textiles (16·6 per cent), machines and tools (14 per cent), means of transport (13·8 per cent), chemical products (7·5 per cent), foodstuffs, drink and tobacco (11·1 per cent), and metals (10·2 per cent).* Unfortunately for Angola, the larger part of the resulting profit margin is appropriated by the colonial administration and a few individuals. Mozambique on the other hand buys more from the metropolis than it sells; but this is all to Portugal's advantage, and in any case the country remains solvent, since it has a substantial source of revenue in South Africa, as we have already seen.

The Portuguese economic system, in fact, represents one of the most conservative and inertia-ridden forms of capitalism, and this is the reason for the economic under-development both of the metropolis and of its Overseas Territories.

The Portuguese colonies are an important source of currency for Portugal, who maintains her liquidity by means of the following system. For some years now the balance of payments of the metropolis has shown a deficit. The reasons for this lie in the constant war expenditures and the constant debts incurred by Portugal in her dealings with other countries. On the other hand the balance of payments of the whole escudo area still shows a constant surplus, thanks to the colonies, whose balance of payments remains in credit and so restores the situation in favour of the metropolis. Large inflows of foreign capital for investments in Angola and Mozambique constitute an important factor in balancing Lisbon's deficit. The *Observer** stated that the trade surplus generated in 1970, amounting to £20 million, had been the main factor in eliminating the trade deficit for Portugal that year. Thus the Portuguese colonies ensure a constant growth in gold reserves and stocks of currency, enabling Portugal to remain internationally solvent and carry on a war on three different colonial fronts.

This role as a provider of hard currency is so important that the Third Quinquennial Plan makes a point of developing it to the utmost. Thus substantial sums will be allotted for the extension of means of communication and transport. For Mozambique, 'funds which are not destined for the ports and railways essential to international communications will be severely reduced'. Cassinga, in Angola, is expected to provide 5 million tons of iron ore per year. Hence the urgent necessity of improving transport facilities. Prospecting rights in the Cassinga ore deposits have belonged since 1961 to a consortium led by Krupps under the control of the Companhia Mineira de Lobita. Since April 1970 a railway line has linked the port of Nacala in Mozambique with Malawi – a country which, because of President Banda, is currently within the 'sphere of influence' of South Africa.

'Assimilation' in theory and practice

One of the more curious characteristics of Portuguese

colonialism as formulated by Dr Salazar is surely the distinction drawn between 'natives' and *assimilados*. In theory, any native who satisfies a certain number of requirements can become *assimilado* or 'civilised', and enjoy the same rights as an ordinary Portuguese citizen. The subject is dealt with in an edict passed on 20 May 1954. Article 2 of this edict defines the status of a native

> Natives of the provinces of Guinea, Angola and Mozambique comprise individuals of the black race or their descendants born or habitually residing in those territories who do not yet possess the education or the individual and social habits which are a prerequisite for the application of the full public and private rights of Portuguese citizens.
>
> Also to be considered as natives are those individuals born of a native father and mother in a place outside these provinces, where the parents are temporarily residing.

There would certainly be nothing dramatic about being born and remaining a 'native' if this concept – which is only meaningful within the context of the Portuguese colonial system – did not imply a number of serious prejudices.

Let us ask, for a moment, what are the rights enjoyed by a native under the 'civilising mission' of the Portuguese.

Firstly on a political level; there are none. Only Portuguese citizens or *assimilados* who have obtained Portuguese citizenship are allowed any means of political self-expression, and even they are more restricted than in Portugal itself. Again, in the sphere of labour legislation, the native's rights are non-existent. He can hardly register a complaint when no machinery exists for his protection. The very existence of forced labour is explained by the fact that the natives have practically no means of resisting it. Perhaps then, there may be some collective or individual rights attributed to the African community or its members? Again, the answer is no.

In fact the 'natives' of the Portuguese colonies are neither citizens nor even subjects, but rather the objects of a predetermined policy. Salazar, who held back the process of 'assimilation' as much as possible and was a great theoretician of colonialism, expressed his ideas clearly enough.

Is the language which we teach superior to their dialects or not? Is the religion spread by the missionaries superior to fetishism or not? Is it better to construct a civilised nation of international weight and significance, or to remain confined by regionalism, without any stimulus towards development, without means of defence or opportunities for progress? If we reply to these questions in the affirmative, then we are forced to the conclusion that this state of national consciousness which the Portuguese have created amongst such a varied group of peoples represents a benefit for all, which we shall lose altogether if we allow ourselves to retreat from our position.

One is born a native, but one has to deserve the status of a Portuguese. Let us therefore examine the conditions which have to be met by anyone who aspires to this 'state of national consciousness' mentioned by Salazar.

According to article 56 of the edict of 20 May 1954

An individual may lose his status as a native and acquire citizenship if he can prove that he satisfies cumulatively the following five conditions:

1 That he is over eighteen years of age.

2 That he speaks the Portuguese language correctly.

3 That he exercises a profession, art or skill from which he can derive sufficient income for his own subsistence and that of persons of his family or persons dependent upon him, or that he possesses sufficient property to fulfil the same purpose.

4 That he is of good behaviour and has acquired the education and habits which are a prerequisite for the

application of the full public and private rights of Portuguese citizens.

5 That he has not been noted as objecting to military service or declared a deserter.

Having fulfilled these conditions an African in the Portuguese colonies '*may* lose his status as a native'. In other words these conditions are absolutely essential, but not necessarily sufficient. The final judgement depends on the discretion of the colonial authority. And the latter will select only useful subjects, who will be future allies or functionaries of the regime.

The first clause, concerning age, means above all that citizenship cannot be passed on from father to son. Each person has to merit it, so that the son of a man who is 'Portuguese by adoption' will still be a 'native' all the same. This situation has become fairly common, moreover, since Salazarism restricted the opportunities for acquiring citizenship. Thus it is easy for the regime to control the numbers of *assimilados* exactly as it wishes, without the process snowballing over the course of generations.

Obviously the second clause, concerning the language, presupposes a sufficient number of primary schools. We have just seen how few schools there were in the Portuguese colonies in 1960. But it is not enough for a young African to have learned to speak Portuguese in one of the elementary schools organised by the Catholic Church. Only the state schools are recognised as being able to teach the language correctly. It goes without saying that the state schools are even fewer in number. Nor is it sufficient to have been through a state school; in the final instance it is left to the administrative authorities to judge whether the aspiring citizen speaks the language correctly or not.

The third clause is reminiscent of the electoral system in nineteenth-century Europe – only a man who has 'possessions', and therefore something to defend, is considered to be a citizen.

The fourth clause brings in the police, who will choose between the good and the bad natives and will only give satisfaction to those who submit to colonial authority without a murmur. This could also explain why there are so few *assimilados* in the Portuguese Overseas Territories. In Angola, in 1960, there were less than 40,000 out of an African population of nearly 5 million, or less than 1 per cent. In Guinea there have never been more than a few hundred.

What advantages does an African gain from holding Portuguese citizenship? In Portugal itself the regime does not allow any political opposition except for a short period during elections. It was not until 1969 that opposition candidates were allowed access to the electoral lists; previously they were reserved exclusively for the candidates of Dr Salazar's party. The opposition has to print its own voting papers, yet neither the official format of these nor the compulsory typographical style are revealed by the government. Once the elections are over the opposition candidates can be prosecuted for unauthorised political activity. In the colonies, the elections are rigged to an even greater extent.

In terms of everyday life, the status of the *assimilado* is in reality no more enviable than that of the native. Admission to the schools is still just as difficult. The *assimilado* does not have the same rights and privileges as the colonists. Since 1937, for instance, the latter have been entitled to an immediate grant of twenty hectares of land worked by Africans, agricultural tools, cattle and a monthly subsidy.

In 1969, Salazar made the following statement:

As the Overseas Territories progress economically and socially, and as the élites become more numerous and effective on a local level, centrifugal forces may appear which aspire to the fullness of power and seek to monopolise situations, and this represents a danger to the unity of the nation. In Portugal's case, the paths to the highest posts are open, and being made ever more easy of access – though born in Spain, Hadrian can become emperor in Rome.

But in vain do we look for the Africans who have acceded to these high offices as promised. Who are the equivalents, in Portuguese Africa, of Felix Eboué and Felix Houphouët-Boigny, or of a Robert Gardiner who was mentioned as a candidate to take over from U Thant at the UN? There is only the African bishop of the kingdom of the Kongo, so often cited by admirers of the regime – and that was some time ago, to say the least. In fact, in 1960 the people of Angola, Guinea and Mozambique were represented in parliament by Europeans. And, apart from this, when 'assimilation' has succeeded, it has invariably entailed a renunciation of the person's original culture. The *assimilados* have had to forget their African traditions, and even their own language. Basil Davidson comments that even 'men such as Cabral, Neto and Mondlane, have also had to take themselves through a systematic process of "reafrican-isation" before they could hope to make progress'.*

It is a high price to pay for the privilege of sharing some of the meagre rights of the Portuguese citizen.

THREE

The Birth of Three Nations

The Armed Struggle

ON 4 February 1961, militants of the *Movimiento Popular de Libertação de Angola* (MPLA) attacked Luanda prison with arms seized from Portuguese soldiers and police, in an attempt to liberate the political prisoners. It was a turning point in the history of the Portuguese colonies in Africa – Africa's Black Mother had given the signal for the wars of liberation.

On 23 January 1963 the armed forces of the *Partido Africano da Independencia de Guiné e Cabo Verde* (PAIGC) invaded the Tite barracks, then started an insurrection in the north and south of the country.

Finally, on 25 September 1964, the *Frente de Libertação de Moçambique* (FRELIMO) appealed to the people of Mozambique in the following terms:

> Workers and peasants, in plantations, sawmills and concessions, in mines, ports and factories, intellectuals, officials, students, soldiers of Mozambique in the Portuguese army, men, women, young people, patriots – today, in your name, the FRELIMO solemnly proclaims to the world the general armed insurrection of the Mozambican people against Portuguese colonialism for the conquest of complete and total independence for their country.

Since this last date, Portugal has been engaged in an

African war on several fronts. Certainly the outbreak of these struggles was not unforeseeable. The first clandestine parties appeared in Angola in 1953. They merged in 1956 to form the MPLA. The PAIGC was already secretly gathering arms and planning tactics in 1956. The FRELIMO was created in 1962 and appointed Professor Eduardo Mondlane as its president in September of the same year.

The creation of these three big movements and the history of their wars will be dealt with in detail. Though they are rich in individual characteristics it may be of interest at this point to single out some of the features they have in common.

First of all, these three movements seem to have brought almost identical social forces into play in the three different countries. The leading part in the preparations for armed struggle was played by a small sector of the middle classes – intellectuals and officials – amalgamated with socially conscious elements within the awakening proletariat. Then the struggle spread to the countryside. The rural petty bourgeoisie rallied to the cause more quickly than their urban counterparts, who are closely dependent on the colonial power and generally gain more social and economic advantages from it. Naturally it is the social groups most directly oppressed by the colonial situation which are the first to see the advantages of independence. But as the struggle also claims to be aiming at a radical transformation of society, a true social revolution, it has inevitably alienated, at least to begin with, numerous traditional chiefs of clan societies who have found their power threatened by the new democratic policies being inaugurated in the liberated zones. In Guinea, for instance, the Portuguese have succeeded in obtaining a kind of benevolent neutrality from a number of traditional chiefs as well as from the more aristocratic families. Likewise the traders have felt threatened by the new organisation of commerce set up in the liberated zones. The petty bourgeoisie has generally been afraid of losing its privileges. The civil servants have obviously remained on the side of the colonial power, though some of them have often done so under instructions from the PAIGC. In the case of Angola, the petty bourgeoisie, more numerous than in Guinea and Mozambique, has provided elements already devoted to nationalism. Another feature of Angola is that exploitation of labour and police repression have ceased.

Now let us take a look at the general characteristics which the three movements have in common. First of all they are 'national fronts', trying to unite the people by mobilising all levels of society against a common enemy – not the Portuguese, but Portuguese 'colonialism'. There are also a number of common features in their political strategies. For instance, as a result of the failure of all legitimate forms of action – strikes, demonstrations, etc. – each of them became convinced of the necessity of armed struggle. In each case the struggle has not been localised but has spread throughout the territory. Although in each of the three countries revolutionary forces are to be found in the towns, guerilla activities all stem from the rural areas. Some urban centres are already harassed by commando attacks. The towns, in many instances penetrated by small clandestine networks, remain the final objective of the struggle. The military and political organisations are not separate but closely interlinked.

Each movement is conscious of having embarked on a war which may last for a long time. It is not a revolt they are engaged in, but a revolution. Its aim is not solely to drive out Portuguese colonialism but also to inaugurate a new society. For this the populations must be aroused to a state of political consciousness, production must be organised on different bases, each country must learn above all to stand on its own feet. Thus, as far as the means and the opportunities for it exist, the armed struggle goes hand in hand with the political struggle.

Needless to say, the three movements are in favour of African unity and non-alignment. Their non-alignment, however, is of a particular kind. In the words of Agostinho Neto: 'It is impossible to wage an effective struggle against the classic form of colonialism without also combating neo-colonialism and imperialism.' Like the leaders of the PAIGC and the FRELIMO, he refuses however, to be caught up in the existing ideological conflicts of the left.

Similarly, at the Tricontinental Conference in Havana in 1966, Amilcar Cabral declared:

If we accept the principle that 'the struggle for liberation is a revolution', and that this struggle does not end the moment the national flag is hoisted and the national anthem played, we shall see that there neither is nor can be any national liberation without the use of liberating violence by the nationalist forces against the criminal violence of the agents of imperialism.

The MPLA, the PAIGC and the FRELIMO seem well equipped to change the *status quo* in Africa. Their leaders already possess a clearer ideology, a military outlook and elements of a genuine experience of democracy in a popular context.

The nationalists of the three countries are also struggling for cooperation between their movements. Their organisations, therefore, joined forces as the Conference of Nationalist Organisations of the Portuguese Colonies (CONCP), founded in 1961 in Rabat and consisting of the PAIGC, the MPLA, the FRELIMO and also the CLSTP, or Committee for the Liberation of São Tomé and Príncipe.

The aims of this combined front are to create a platform for the struggle against the common enemy, to exchange combat experiences, to take up similar political positions with regard to African and international problems, and finally to coordinate the different movements' activities.

The CONCP has an executive council presided over in turn by each of the leaders of its member movements. Special committees deal with problems of political, military or cultural coordination.

The three organisations also have links with the nationalist movements in racialist countries such as South Africa, Rhodesia and Namibia.

But how 'communist' are the Liberation Movements?

The question here is certainly not to answer Pretoria and Lisbon, who will call anyone 'communist', who is not in agreement with extreme right-wing theories. Perhaps the best answer to this question was given by Amilcar Cabral when receiving in Conakry, on 7 January 1971, a delegation of the International Union of Students – IUS:

To beat the Portuguese is not a cause for pride for us. It would be a great cause of pride for us to liberate our country and to get independence and to build the progress of our people. This is the fundamental reason for the fight and in this way we try each day more to give more political conscience to our people, the people in the countryside, the militants in general, the fighters, and all persons in leadership positions. We are organising many seminars, meetings, conferences at which we can discuss all problems directly concerning our people, Africa and the world. Naturally Salazar, his substitute Caetano and the Portuguese in general as well as some of the western press present us as great terrorists and communists paid by Moscow, Peking, Havana, and so on. We think that if really being a communist means to fight for the independence of one's country, for freedom and for the right to progress, then this is very good propaganda for communism. This is our opinion. But we know in our country that we are fighting for our independence. And the first condition in this fight is to be independent in our thought and in our action.

Angola, Africa's Black Mother

The Origins of the Struggle and the MPLA

> There are fifty thousand dead for whom no one has wept
> No one ...
> The mothers of Angola
> Fell with their children.
>
> *Fernando Costa Andrade*

The war of liberation in Angola has two distinguishing features – it was the first to begin, and it has been the bloodiest.

On 4 February 1961 the militants of the MPLA attacked a police patrol. Having seized their weapons, they made their way to various police stations. A number of them made for the Luanda prison, intending to free the political prisoners, who included several MPLA leaders. The operation was unsuccessful, but it made a strong impression on the Angolan people. Too many Africans and militants had passed through the prisons of Angola, and particularly that in Luanda, for the population not to take an interest in any attempt to overthrow them. Successful or not, it was an attack on the very symbol of oppression.

During the following two days 3,000 people were executed in Luanda. A few days later came the massacre at Baixo de Cassange in which 5,000 people met their deaths. The militants took refuge in the forests in the north-west of Angola. After this date, the Angolan rebellion was still to suffer a number of internal disputes, but the signal for concerted action had now been given. The day of 4 February 1961 was in fact the historic moment which marked the beginning of the insurrection.

Going Outside the Law

The actual idea of resistance is very much older than

this, however, and the Angolan nationalist movement, which dates from the beginning of the century, is the oldest on the black continent.

There are several examples of earlier resistance which could be mentioned. Around the turn of the century and up to 1910, a group of intellectuals – Silverio Pereira, Paixão Franco, Cordeira de Matta, Assis Junior and many others – denounced colonialism and laid the bases of an Angolan nationalist movement.

In the twenties, the country was completely dominated by Portugal. In 1929 the African National League began to talk of the necessity of going outside the law in order to fight the Portuguese colonial system. Resistance then appeared in a number of different forms. In the towns, it created several movements, some of them literary, which gave expression to the rebellion and sought to mobilise the people against the Portuguese.

This political and cultural movement then expanded and spread into the countryside. It became necessary to create specific political organisations which would speak in the name of Angola and struggle against the restricted allegiances of the different tribes. Around 1950 agitation increased in the towns, inscriptions appeared on the walls, and the nation's youth began to become involved. It was also at this point that the PIDE – the Portuguese political police – made its appearance in Angola, set up its networks and informers, and began making mass arrests. In 1953 small clandestine movements began to appear. The MPLA, created on 10 December 1956, stemmed from these movements and, in particular, from the Party for the United Struggle of the Angolan Africans (PLUA), and the Movement for the National Independence of Angola (MINA). By 1960 the MPLA was convinced that only revolutionary violence could put an end to colonialism, and began to organise armed groups.

On 29 March 1959, the political police made a series of arrests; dozens of militants or suspected militants were imprisoned. A month later, on 26 April, the Portuguese Air Force arrived in Angola. The Governor-General explained their appearance as follows: 'Angola is not in a state of peace and harmony.... The country will be undefended unless we set up a military organisation.' In July 1959 a new series of arrests took in several leaders of the MPLA, including Ilidio Machado. On 8 June 1960 it was the turn of Dr Agostinho Neto, then honorary president of the MPLA, to be arrested. The inhabitants of two villages in his native region, Icolo and Bengo, rebelled, and thirty people were killed and 200 wounded as a result. On 25 June of the same year the wave of arrests overtook another MPLA leader – Father Joaquim Pinto de Andrade, now honorary president of the MPLA, a doctor of theology, Chancellor of the Archbishopric of Luanda and a member of the Executive Council of the Society of African Culture. Militants were being interrogated daily, and usually tortured in the process. The army was increasing its acts of intimidation, raiding villages and burning the houses of suspects. On 29 December 1960 about twenty nationalists, mostly from the Cabinda district, were executed in the courtyard of Luanda prison.

This systematic repression resulted in the partial destruction of the movement's networks in the interior of the country, and more generally in the loss of a large number of its most active militants, whose absence was cruelly felt in March 1961 when the armed struggle broke out. One of the most critical areas of revolutionary activity was the north of the country, where a movement known as the Union of the Peoples of Angola (UPA) had established itself, based largely on the exploitation of tribal rivalries.

Counter-Revolutionary Movements

Created in 1958 from the break-up of the Union of the Peoples of North Angola (UPNA), this organisation had no real political doctrine; its main objective was opposition to the MPLA. As its leader said later to Robert Davezies:

'I have emphasised the political education of our people, but we have to draw on our own experience, taking into account the difficulties and the circumstances which we find in our path. We have not found a political formula.'*

Some of the UPA's slogans show fairly clearly what form this education took:

'Kill all the whites, all those of mixed blood, all intellectuals and all the militants of the MPLA'; 'kill everything white'; 'smoke *diamba* [hashish] to be able to fight more fiercely'; 'make fetishes so as to be invulnerable to bullets'.*

The UPA had indeed taken up arms, but certainly not for the purpose of revolution. Its recruitment was based on feelings such as tribalism, religious intolerance and hatred of intellectuals.

In March 1961 a savage rebellion took place in the district of Uige and the surrounding regions, during which several hundred European civilians perished. This outbreak, which was linked with the Bakongo rising, may be looked upon as one of the consequences of the events in Luanda. Although there can be no doubt of the spontaneity of the massacre, the UPA cannot be entirely absolved of responsibility for it, since its influence on the Bakongo had always been very great. Whatever the truth of the matter, this massacre of Europeans resulted in heavy reprisals by the Portuguese, and the death of more than 20,000 Africans, according to figures supplied by English baptist missionaries.

On more than one occasion, the militants of the UPA massacred individuals or groups who refused to enter their ranks, or combatants of the MPLA.

On 3 March 1962 the former UPA leader, Marcos Kassanga, gave a press conference in Kinshasa – then still Leopoldville – during which he stated:

The fight which has broken out in the north of Angola is a truly fratricidal war. Around 8,000 Angolans have been savagely massacred by tribalist elements of the UPA, who have stupidly been armed and are totally lacking in discipline. This inhuman massacre of Angolans by Angolans is the result of blind tribalism.

And in June 1968, in a broadcast on Radio Tanzania, Agostinho Neto declared: 'In this way we have lost thousands of men, women and children, all of whom would have made sincere patriots and ardent fighters for the cause of national liberation.'

Thus, torn by internal dissension, the national liberation movement was a sitting target for the Portuguese counter-offensive. A series of extremely violent operations were launched in August and September 1961, resulting in 50,000 dead and 300,000 refugees.

The question arises as to whether the UPA was a tool of the CIA. Observers have noted that it received large quantities of weapons and financial support from the United States. Financial aid was supposedly given on the condition that the UPA did not join forces with the MPLA, or any of the fronts in which the MPLA played a part.

For three years the MPLA and the UPA waged a wholesale war against one another, on the pattern of the FLN and the Messalites in Algeria. In 1961 the MPLA's troops were decimated. But they had to reach the interior of the country, and send columns to the north. The group commanded by Tomas Ferreira was massacred in this way in the region of Fuesse. At the same time, the UPA was strengthening its position on an international level.

On 27 March 1962 the UPA and the PDA – formerly ALIAZO* – founded the National Liberation Front of Angola, the FNLA. Established in Leopoldville in 1963 the UPA created the Revolutionary Government of Angola in Exile (GRAE), which was immediately recognised by Cyrille Adoula, the president of the Congo. It was around this time that a group of combatants of the MPLA were intercepted near the frontier by the Congolese authorities.

On 2 November 1963 the government of the Congo-Kinshasa banned the MPLA from its territory. This prohibition is still in force today and even the medical services of the MPLA were ousted from the country.

The MPLA was therefore considerably weakened by these diplomatic and military setbacks. But the far-reaching programme of political activity did not cease, and this long period of hardship only served to strengthen the will of the militants and to provide the movement with its most effective cadres – a fact which was demonstrated by the Conference of Cadres held in Brazzaville in 1964. At this conference Agostinho Neto was re-elected president of the movement, and his policies and moral authority were doubly confirmed. When the MPLA opened the Cabinda front in 1964, the crisis could be considered as over. In addition, the GRAE was torn by internal dissension and it lost the support of the Tshombe government. Before long – on 25 November 1964 – the MPLA was recognised by the Organisation of African Unity (OAU). In 1969 the Military Commission of the OAU inspected a liberated region in Angola. After journeying hundreds of kilometres escorted by the MPLA and returning to Addis Ababa, the commission was convinced that the day was not far off when the guerillas would reach the shores of the Atlantic.

In 1966 another counter-revolutionary group, the UNITA or *União Nacional por la Independencia Total de Angola* – a movement with tribal and racial overtones – tried to infiltrate certain regions of Angola including the Moxico and Bié districts, and organised a few military actions against the Portuguese, most of which met with failure.

UNITA and GRAE both claim to be revolutionary. But, says Agostinho Neto: 'Violence is not always revolutionary. There is another form which is reactionary, and we can tell one from the other. We are not likely to confuse Hitler with Ho Chi Minh.'*

Cabinda, Laboratory of the Revolution

This dispersion of strength was more decisive on a diplomatic level than in terms of what was actually happening inside the country. In fact, from 1964 onwards the MPLA was the only party fighting against the Portuguese military forces. This situation began in the enclave of Cabinda, over the northern frontier, which was brought into the war around 1964. Before this date, the MPLA had found it difficult to organise the rebellion from the Congo-Brazzaville republic, since Fulbert Youlou's government, having ties with France and Portugal, was hostile to the movement. After 1963, with the triumph of revolution in the Congo, activities could once more be organised from there. As a result it was impossible to attack the small district of Cabinda, covering about 7,000 square kilometres and scarcely fifty kilometres across, even though it was occupied by substantial numbers of Portuguese troops.

The opening of the Cabinda Front was a move of decisive importance. A revolutionary training centre was established there and has produced most of the current commanders of the guerilla troops. Cabinda was the school, the 'laboratory' of the Angolan revolution. In addition, the war and subsequent victory in the province of Cabinda had a strong psychological impact on the Angolan people. They restored the masses' confidence in the MPLA and in the possibility of victory over the Portuguese army. It is now generally conceded that the Angolan war of liberation started in Cabinda.

After Cabinda, it was two years before another front was opened. This was the Eastern Front. In 1965, Agostinho Neto obtained permission from Zambia and Tanzania to open supply routes to the east of Angola. This assistance from the two governments was decisive. After two years of effort, the MPLA succeeded in opening the Eastern Front in 1966. The first area to be affected was Moxico, then came the district of Lunda in 1968, then the district of Bié in

1969. In 1970, the MPLA's military operations reached the western bank of the river Cuanza.

This time, the war could be described as a national one, since it embraced practically all the large ethnic groupings. The preponderance of Kimbundu half-breeds among the cadres tended to disappear. Even some of the Bakongo, who had hitherto remained faithful to the UPA, fought beside Mundas, Luchazis and Nengus – all natives of Moxico. In the north-east most of the active elements were Lundas and Chokwes.

The Eastern Front, situated in the dispossessed areas of Eastern Angola, came as a surprise to the colonial authorities. Work was begun on the political education of the inhabitants and then, on 18 May 1966, the first Portuguese patrol was ambushed; by this time it was clear to everyone that the action was not going to stop there.

In 1966, therefore, Agostinho Neto had launched his movement on the right track. The UPA was discredited. The MPLA had recognised its tactical errors, renewed its contacts with the people and emerged both practically and theoretically better armed for the fight, and better able to resist any disruptive forces in its midst. As its leader, Agostinho Neto was clearly a personality of the stature demanded by such an important enterprise. Basil Davidson recently compared him as he was in 1962 and as he is now:

He was an austere, taciturn man, who had the threatening realities of the combat clearly in perspective – the distant outcome, the necessity for total commitment, the obligation to exercise his authority, and against this, the equally imperious obligation to exercise it without yielding to personal ambition. Today he is still austere and sparing in his use of words, but his personality has become more flexible, and the years of struggle and hardship have increased his stature. Incontrovertibly, he dominates the MPLA but he does so with modesty and humour. Though he prevails over everyone else, he considers that this confers on him not privileges but heavier responsibilities.*

Under the leadership of Agostinho Neto, the MPLA has forged its doctrine and its internal organisation. Like the PAIGC and FRELIMO, its doctrine is that of an independent, native, non-racialist, revolutionary movement, struggling for a new society.

Life on the Eastern Front

On 18 May 1966 the MPLA opened its third battle front in the eastern, or third, region. The third region, with an area of 391,000 square kilometres, is four times as large as Portugal, more than two-thirds the size of France or the two Vietnams put together. This comparison indicates the importance of the territory which was at stake, and also the absurdity of Portuguese propaganda claims that 'terrorists with bases abroad are infiltrating into Angola, setting up ambushes and then withdrawing again'.

The third region is a vast plateau 1,000 metres above sea level, sloping slightly to the south-east, crossed by numerous rivers and covered with a vast savannah or *chana* interspersed with forests. It was in this area that the guerillas established themselves, using all the resources of the terrain.

During the rainy season the savannah is flooded. The soil is a sort of sandy clay in which sorghum and millet can easily be grown. Rice was originally grown here as a colonial crop, destined for export, but is now no longer cultivated. The rivers are extremely rich in fish, which are the region's principal source of protein. Another source of food are the two game reserves created by the Portuguese – Cameia in the north and Chitengé in the south. Bee-keeping is a traditional activity and provides large quantities of honey, which in former times was carried to the ports by caravans of slaves. Today, honey is used as a secondary source of protein for regions which are poor in fish. The Portuguese also gained considerable revenue from the wood in the forests of Moxico but this is, of course, no longer exploited. In fact this region, like the rest of Angola, is poor in sources of food and is suffering from the effects of colonial exploitation.

Perhaps for this reason, the third region is sparsely inhabited. The population numbers around 38,000, i.e. one inhabitant per square kilometre, and is composed of a number of different tribes – the Chokwes, Luvales, Lundas, Mbundas, Luchazis, Kangalas and Kwanglis, who are mostly shepherds, and the Khoi-San, who are hunters. Vast areas are practically depopulated, in particular the Cuando Cubango district.

These people, who today live under the banner of the MPLA, are organised into 'action committees', whose leaders are elected directly by the population. Thus it would seem that the bases of a genuinely democratic system have been laid. For example, a former traditional chief – known as the *soba* – may or may not be elected by his former subjects. In addition – and this is very important – families belonging to different ethnic groups are settling in new villages built to meet the requirements of the war, and this is helping to break down the old tribal barriers.

One remarkable aspect of the MPLA's activities in the liberated zones is the sanitary and medical assistance which has been made available. Since 1963 the Angolan people have had a proper Medical Aid Service (SAM) at their disposal, which has been established in all the five military regions – the 1st (or northern) region, covering the districts of Luanda, Uige, Cuanza Norte and Zaïre; the 2nd region – Cabinda; the 3rd region – Moxico and Cuando Cubango; the 4th region – Lunda and Malanje; and the 5th, connected with the district of Bié.

Each region is administered by a doctor and divided up into several zones, each managed by a medical aide; and each zone is divided in turn into sectors, with a nurse or assistant nurse at their head. Which demonstrates SAM's need for qualified personnel.

An elementary medical school disseminates basic information on anatomy, first aid and hygiene. A fairly rudimentary hospital functions in the second region. The other regions are even more poorly provided for, though there are a number of camouflaged travelling dispensaries which give first aid to the wounded in the interior of the country.

For quite a long time now the third region has ceased to be a combat area, being decisively controlled by MPLA forces. Guerilla activities continue elsewhere. In the words of Agostinho Neto:

> Cuanda Cubango and Moxico at present constitute a firm base for the military and political training of the guerillas; the people there lead a near-normal life under war conditions and give great support to the combatants who are even further off....*

At the same time as the Eastern Front was being liberated, the Northern Front, hitherto held by the UPA, was undergoing a radical transformation. The disastrous setbacks caused by the encouragement of tribalism, fetishism and tribal hatreds, and the practice of making frontal attacks on the Portuguese troops without any cover, had provided a bitter lesson for the best elements of the movement, who initially took refuge in the forests. Then, under the influence of the MPLA, a fighting front was gradually built up again. Frontal attacks were abandoned in favour of ambushes, and a new form of organisation replaced the non-political 'bands' of fighters. The Cienfuegos column succeeded in secretly crossing the Congo-Kinshasa to the northern region, where it was received with popular rejoicing. Finally, in March 1967, the Kami column followed the same route successfully. The Portuguese blockade of the north-western region was thus twice broken, and the population, who had been left to their fate since 1961, regained confidence in the struggle. But clearly, the Portuguese circle around the north-west region has still to be shaken.

Extending the Armed Struggle

Thus, at the beginning of 1967, Agostinho Neto was able to announce 'the extension of the armed struggle throughout the whole of the national territory'. And at a press conference in Brazzaville on 3 January 1968, he stated: 'Other regions will be affected this year, so that there will no longer be isolated battle fronts, but a single, continuous front which will engulf the enemy, paralyse him and render him harmless.'

A new phase of the struggle was beginning. On 8 May 1968 a fourth front was opened in the north-east of Angola, in the regions of Lunda and Malanje. On 6 June 1969 it was the turn of the Bié district.

Of course the war has had its losses as well as its victories, and on 14 April 1968, the MPLA lost one of its most glorious fighters, José Mendes de Carvalho, otherwise Comrade Henda, who at the age of twenty-six had become the senior commander of the war in Angola. The story of his career recalls the early years of the MPLA's military organisation. Henda went underground at the age of seventeen and was soon being sought by the PIDE. He took refuge in the Congo-Kinshasa, where he became a member of the first group of Angolan patriots to become organised on a military basis abroad. He returned to Angola in January 1961 and organised the underground movement in Cabinda in 1964. While carrying out a mission in Northern Rhodesia – then under the British – he was arrested by the British police and condemned to hard labour. He regained his freedom at the time of Zambian independence. In 1966 Henda, who was now twenty-four, was made responsible for the movement's military organisation throughout the national territory. The Eastern Front was created. Then Henda was killed while leading an attack by the 4th Section on the Karipande barracks – one of the last Portuguese posts isolated on the borders of the third region. On this subject, Agostinho Neto explained later:

To those who say that we should spare our cadres, that they should not expose themselves physically in the fighting, that they should spare their lives, their health or their freedom because they will be needed in the Angola of tomorrow, for the survival of the Movement, I would say that the national war of liberation cannot be waged without cadres; that every cadre who is trained, whatever his personality, must be able to work inside the country, in order to make his contribution to solving the problems of the struggle and of national reconstruction. That is the only just and revolutionary attitude.

At the first assembly of the MPLA held in the third region, in the district of Moxico, the executive committee was able to announce that a third of the national territory was controlled by the MPLA and that nine of the fifteen districts mapped out by the colonial administration – Cabinda, Zaïre, Uige, Cuanza Norte, Lunda, Moxico, Bié and Cuando Cubango – were in a state of war.

Since then several of the MPLA's theoretical objectives seem to have been attained, or at least to be well on the way to it. First of all, the national revolution is now directed from the interior – the headquarters of the MPLA are established inside the country and not abroad. Agostinho Neto leads the movement, assisted by a 'political and military coordination committee', which is supposed to meet every year. The executive committee itself is subordinate to MPLA assemblies, organised by local action committees at village level.

Obviously this structure does not function with clockwork-like regularity. Indeed the rigours of war prevent it from doing so most of the time. Nevertheless, contact with the population is never sacrificed to the demands of authority, and great freedom of decision is maintained at a local level.

As a matter of general policy the war is to be extended throughout the national territory and encircle the towns which, having been undermined secretly from the inside, should eventually fall in the final phase of the war. The politico-military aspect of the war is also constantly underlined, both in the MPLA's contact with and organisation of the population, and in the training of cadres, who are selected and educated according to political as well as military criteria. Finally, it goes without saying that the MPLA's war of liberation is profoundly national in character, rising above tribal divisions and disputes. In this area also, the movement is constantly working for the country's political education.

Guinea Bissao, A Practically Liberated Country

The Origins of the Struggle and the PAIGC

> That year ... we decided to create our Party secretly.
> That is to say that our climactic moment before the
> armed struggle is when we arrived at the conviction that
> it was not possible to work unless it was underground.*

That year was 1956, and it was in September that Amilcar
Cabral secretly founded the PAIGC in Bissao with a handful of his comrades. Before that date, says Cabral, they had
founded 'recreational organisations', i.e. sporting or cultural
organisations which were non-political in character. Now,
even these organisations had been forbidden, which demonstrated to the youth of Guinea Bissao that it had practically
no rights at all and that 'assimilation' was a complete sham.

The three years from 1956 to 1959 were taken up with
group discussions held in total secrecy, in order to try to
formulate theoretical problems and a plan of action among
the urban masses.

In the meantime, the Portuguese government had produced a new weapon in the form of the Portuguese political
police, the PIDE, some of whom were transferred to Guinea
Bissao. On 3 August 1959 they put down a strike at the
port of Pijiguiti; fifty people were killed.

Two facts now became clear to the leaders of the PAIGC.
Firstly that their efforts of the past three years were beginning to bear fruit, since as a result of the Pijiguiti massacre
all the small clandestine groups were now uniting around a
single party – the PAIGC. And secondly that the political
line they had followed hitherto was a mistake. So far they
had aimed to pursue the struggle in the towns by means of
exemplary activities such as strikes and demonstrations,
relying simultaneously on the support of the proletariat
which, emerging from the rural exodus and the petty

bourgeoisie, had been disappointed by assimilation. But the towns were Portuguese strongholds where the PIDE could manoeuvre with ease.

In September 1959, therefore, a month after the events at Pijiguiti, a secret meeting of the Party was held in Bissao. This was an important turning point in so far as it was then decided to carry the main effort of the movement into the countryside in order to create there the conditions for the armed struggle. 'At the moment the Party knew nothing of what was happening in the world and we had to advance empirically.'*

From 1959 a substantial number of PAIGC leaders, such as Rafael Barbosa, its future president, left for the *mato*, in the forests, in order to set up the Party's basic organisation. Numerous militants from the towns took to the *maquis*, going from village to village in order to prepare the peasants for guerilla warfare. Guinea Bissao was divided into six regions and into operational zones. In 1960 the Party was hit by repression and Amilcar Cabral had to go into exile in Conakry.

In August 1961, after the MPLA's attack on Luanda prison, the PAIGC decided to coordinate the struggle with that in Angola by a series of direct actions in Guinea Bissao itself. Sabotage by the militants was met with savage repression by the Portuguese. About twenty members of the PAIGC, including its president Rafael Barbosa, Fernando Fortes, Epifanio and numerous others, were arrested. This ordeal seems chiefly to have confirmed the PAIGC in its political orientation, stimulated the courage of its combatants and implanted the idea of struggle firmly in their minds.

At the end of July 1962, 3,000 people were arrested in Bissao and a state of siege was declared. In August 1962 an important conference of Party cadres was held, and finally, in January 1963, the armed struggle began in the south of the country. 'Numerous well armed groups, trained in subversive warfare in North Africa and the Communist countries, have penetrated Guinean territory,' declared the Portuguese minister of defence. By this time a third of the country was already infiltrated by the guerillas.

The Reaction at Different Social Levels

Let us consider for a moment which of the social strata in 1961 were most likely to be affected by these developments. First of all in the towns.

There are five important towns in Guinea Bissao; their population consists of about 300 Portuguese, a handful of *assimilados* (originally from the Cape Verde Islands, holding high official positions which carry with them a certain amount of power), and a petty bourgeoisie consisting of civil servants, white-collar workers and small traders, whose political attitude swings between total support of the Portuguese and a desire to see them driven out so that they may take their place as leaders of the country. It was this middle class which provided the leaders of the struggle for liberation. But it also feeds the ranks of the political police, the PIDE. Finally there are the wage-earners or manual workers, numbering around 30,000, who were quick to lend their support to the struggle. Together with the country's youth, they have often been a source of Party cadres. The sub-proletariat in the towns, on the other hand, is difficult to reach and most of the time is infiltrated by the political police, who recruit their informers from it.

Rural society in Guinea Bissao has two distinguishing features – forced labour does not exist, and the peasants are in possession of the land. Unlike Angola and Mozambique, there has been no exodus of young, able-bodied men who have been forced to leave their villages to go and work in the mines. The structure of the rural community has therefore remained fairly stable. In addition the Portuguese have never succeeded in depopulating large areas in order to install Portuguese smallholders, or create vast plantations. The Guineans have therefore been able to keep their land, which is generally owned collectively by the village.

'We speak of peasants, but the term "peasant" is very vague. The peasant who fought in Algeria or China is not the peasant of our country,' writes Amilcar Cabral.*

In fact rural Guinea Bissao today is divided basically into two groups – on the one hand are the animist Balantas, numbering about 25,000, who joined the struggle from the very beginning; on the other are the Muslim Fulahs, whose leaders and great noble families have been devoted to the Portuguese since the beginning of colonisation. The Portuguese set up Muslim chiefs over the Balantas, who are mostly peasants. The latter were often doubly exploited, both by their chiefs and by the Portuguese, who regularly came to levy taxes in kind. Today, in the words of the Portuguese. 'The Fulahs are our right arm.'* Together with the other Muslim groups they make up some 35 to 40 per cent of the Guinean population. Their social structures, which are preserved and encouraged by the Portuguese, remain semi-feudal, and their chief means of subsistence is by trade.

Of the urban social classes and the peasantry it is the former which have played the more decisive role:

> We can affirm that our peasant is not in any way a primary revolutionary element.... We found the principal revolutionary force in the urban milieu, as much among the petty bourgeois class which was conscious of the foreign domination in our country as among the salaried workers of the ports, the ships, the repair shops, etc.*

The Theoretical School in Conakry

Chiefly because of the small area of territory involved in comparison with Angola and Mozambique, the PAIGC was better able to put its political theories into practice than the other national liberation movements. Nearly six years were spent studying the particular features of Portuguese exploitation in Guinea, in drawing practical conclusions from this study, and in spreading propaganda amongst the villagers.

The real theoretical work, which was to lead to an original concept of anti-colonial revolution in Guinea Bissao, began in Conakry in 1960. Amilcar Cabral, and a few other leaders in exile, created a sort of political school under very poor conditions. Young militants from the towns were the first to come, then young peasants, and recently mobilised soldiers who sometimes arrived with their families. For one or two months they held discussions in groups of twenty-five, sometimes continuing from morning till night. They were not trying to teach or be taught, but to seek together a political line which would take into account the specific circumstances of the country. Quasi-dramatic methods were often used in order to represent as concretely as possible all the components of Guinean society – religion, traditions, tribal divisions – and the possible re-actions of the peasantry to the armed struggle.

Concrete examples were used, such as:

'Did you pay the tax? Did your father pay the tax? What have you seen from that tax? How much do you get from your peanuts? Have you thought about what you will earn with your peanuts? How much sweat has it cost your family?... You are going to work in road-building. Who gives you the tools? You bring the tools. Who provides the meal? You provide the meal. But – who walks in the street? Who has a car?...'*

At all times there was this same insistence on starting from concrete bases, on avoiding theoretical discourses, especially in discussions with the peasants. The peasant had to discover the truth for himself, in the course of the dis-cussion. No one had the right to impose this truth on him or give him lessons. Also, militants had to be sent into the countryside who were capable of becoming totally inte-grated into village life, so that the peasants would then take it upon themselves to convince those around them.

A searching analysis of Guinean social structures was also made at the Conakry school. The leaders of the PAIGC were able to discover which sectors of the population to approach first, with what arguments, and with what objectives.

For this purpose tribal problems – which were and still are important – had to be taken into account. The tribe had to be respected, not as an economic unit, since it no longer was one, but as a cultural unit. Its language and customs were different from those of the next tribe, and this had to be considered, but without allowing tribal allegiances to crystallise, for instance, within the ranks of the army. To avoid encouraging such situations, the head of a detachment was generally of a different tribe from the majority of the men.

The religious beliefs of individuals also had to be respected, though of course the soldiers had to be made to understand that a well-dug trench offered more protection than an amulet.

The second major theoretical stage of the revolution in Guinea was inaugurated at the Congress held in 1964, with the aim of drawing conclusions from the struggles which had already taken place and setting out a plan for the future. By 1964 the movement was well established in the south of the country; relatively autonomous groups of guerillas, linked directly to the head of the Party, were to be found in Cobucaré, Indjassan, Quinara, Quitáfine, and Sususa. The Congress took severe disciplinary measures to deal with some of the guerilla leaders who had become too independent. Most of the political decisions taken are still valid today; amongst them were the following:

- Zones and regions would be created, and the Party fused completely with the army.
- Each zone or region would be directed by a Party member who was also the commander of the guerilla group.
- Guerilla bases would be established outside the villages

and not within them as they had been at first, so that
the character of village life would not be changed and
the peasants would not be subjected to Portuguese repression.
- The Party's Armed Forces would be backed up by an
armed people's militia.
- The regions would be so arranged that they could take
the place of the economic and administrative organisations of the Portuguese.

The Military Situation

After the Congress of 1964 the military situation developed rapidly. The struggle was opened up on two new
fronts – Gabú in the east and Boé in the west. As the
guerillas progressed the Portuguese were forced to draw
back into the urban centres and fortify their posts. The
whole military strategy of the armed forces lies in forcing
the Portuguese to concentrate their resources and confine
themselves in fortified situations isolated both from one another and from the big towns. Today there are three battle
fronts: the Northern Front, the Southern Front and the
Eastern Front.

By 1965 half of the total area of the country was liberated
territory. Since then the Portuguese have used all possible
means of retaliation – the bombing of villages, raids by
helicopter-borne troops, napalm used against crops and
men, combined operations by air, land and sea or river,
psychological operations designed to frighten the people,
break up ethnic groups and win over their chiefs with the
offer of privileges, the use of radio propaganda claiming
that the PAIGC is a Communist movement fighting against
rebellion, the distribution of leaflets in the villages showing, for instance, hungry guerillas in rags with the caption:
'São gente bruta que não vive – que na mata' – 'They are
no more than savages living in the forest.'

Since 1968 substantial reinforcements have been sent by
Lisbon to Guinea Bissao; the country is occupied by 30,000

men commanded by General Spinola, an old-fashioned militarist right down to his monocle. Even the Portuguese admit that what they term 'uninhabited territories' cover 44 per cent of the country. These are designated 'intervention zones' and subjected to frequent bombing. All of which seems a fairly clear admission that they are controlled by the Guinean Armed Forces. Two Portuguese bases, at Beli and Ganture, have been closed. 'We closed them because it was costing too much to keep them supplied with beer,' said one of General Spinola's aides.*

In the past few years, the armed forces have attacked the towns of Bafatá, Gabú, Farim, Manŝoa, Cansumbó and Bolama, and Bissao airport. Today the PAIGC seems to be concentrating its efforts on two objectives – harassing the urban centres, and gaining a footing in the Cape Verde Islands, which are wholly dominated by the Portuguese, who consider them strategically important. In the words of Amilcar Cabral: 'The day the action spreads to the Cape Verde Islands, the struggle will be practically over.'

The Economy, a Second Front

Parallel to, but by no means less important than the military war, is the economic war. This consists basically of two aspects – a negative aspect, which is the systematic sabotage and destruction of the colonial economy; and a positive aspect, which is the construction of a new economy founded on the needs of the population and the combatants.

Sabotage of the Portuguese economic system started in 1963, in a variety of different forms. In January 1963 the inhabitants of the southern-central and southern parts of the country began a total boycott of the Portuguese traders. To avoid the need for fuel, bush fires were maintained for cooking food, and were placed at the disposal of the surrounding villages. The Portuguese trading posts south of the River Corubal were forced to close one by one, except for those supplying the Portuguese colony. The shops of the Companhia União Fabril (CUF), the 'Overseas Commercial Company', and the Mario Lima Whanon and Manuel Pinto Brandão companies were closed in Cacine, Como, São João, Cadigue and Caiar. All their goods were inventoried and seized by the Liberation Army. In 1964 the sabotage increased. In July the guerillas blew up shops belonging to the colonial companies in Buta. In the same year the powerful 'Overseas Commercial Company' closed its trading posts, dismissed its employees and went into liquidation. The biggest of the colonial companies, the CUF, also had to close down a number of its establishments. Since 1965 the CUF has only kept open its trading posts – on the orders of the government – for the use of Portuguese soldiers and officials.

The crops produced by the large plantations were also boycotted. After the campaign of 1963-4, production of ground-nuts, for instance, showed a 50 per cent decrease, enabling the peasants in the liberated zones to increase the area of land devoted to the cultivation of foodstuffs. Supplies to the towns held by the Portuguese were blockaded, and the latter were compelled to import large quantities of rice, even though the rural regions were producing more than they needed.

Commerce was seriously affected by attacks on the colony's communications network. A famous example is the capture of the Portuguese lighter *Persistente*, loaded with goods and provisions destined for Belanda. In 1964 twelve boats were seized and confiscated by the combatants of the PAIGC; communications by road were more or less completely cut off. The ground-nut crop was blockaded in the local *cercos* and warehouses, preventing it from reaching the ports of Bissao and Binta. In 1966 the road from Bissao to Manŝoa was cut off by ambushes, and road and river traffic was seriously disrupted.

Another feature of the systematic sabotage of the colonial economy was the financial and monetary blockade. The use of Portuguese currency was forbidden in the liberated regions, and limited by the commercial boycott in the rest of the country. The majority of the peasantry considered themselves absolved of all debts owed to the colonists, and a large part of the population refused to pay its taxes.

In the liberated regions measures then had to be taken to supply the wants of the combatants and the rest of the population. A new economic system had to be born out of the ashes of the colonial economy. To achieve this several different methods were adopted, the first being an increase in the production of rice – the staple diet of the Guinean population. From the 1963-4 campaign onwards, efforts in this direction began to show promising results. South of Geba the area devoted to rice production was increased from 22,000 to 25,000 hectares, and the average yield was increased from 5 to 15 per cent. In one year, rice production was increased by 15 to 20 per cent. It may be added that these results were obtained in spite of bombing, the deportation of peasants and assassinations of workers in the rice fields. For the first time, the peasants were discovering that they could organise their own work freely, without falling into debt with the Portuguese colonists.

In regions where the population traditionally cultivated other crops, however, the results were less promising, and there was even a shortage of food, compensated for by provisions brought from more favoured regions. Production of manioc, sweet potatoes, haricot beans, millet, leguminous crops and other foodstuffs showed an overall increase, and fruit cultivation was encouraged. In 1966 large quantities of rice could be stockpiled. In 1969 seed-distributions were carried out and the population learned to defend their harvests against bombing with high explosives or napalm.

Another problem was the repair and replacement of agricultural implements. From 1963 this task was taken over by local craftsmen. Village blacksmiths learned to repair and make new tools, and even household utensils such as knives and spoons, with the metal from bombs dropped on the rural centres.

Then *armazens do povo*, 'people's shops', run directly by the PAIGC, were opened in the liberated regions to supply the most urgently needed articles and dispose of the agricultural produce given in return. These shops do not take any money, existing purely to exchange consumer goods for merchandise produced by the people. Although they were welcomed by the population, broken communications have caused problems both in supplying them and in disposing of the goods they collect. Also, exports from the liberated areas are as yet insufficient to match the population's need for foreign products.

Finally, this new popular economy has been accompanied by experiments in new working relationships. In Guinea Bissao the land is generally owned collectively by the tribes, and the question of land reform has therefore never really arisen. But there are other problems:

> Independence is not only a question of driving out the Portuguese, of having a flag and a national anthem. The people must be sure that no one is going to steal the fruits of their labours. That the country's wealth will not find its way into someone else's pocket. Today the people of Guinea are naked. They are still afraid of the river, the rain, the forest. We say to them that through their work the river will be made use of. The object of our struggle is to ensure that the people will have work by which they can feed and clothe themselves, work to provide hospitals and schools for the children. It is for this that the Party exists. It is for this that we have taken up arms and will drive out the Portuguese.*

It should be noted that the situation is not the same in the Cape Verde Islands, where the cultivable land is divided up into large plantations. Even in Guinea Bissao, however, the development and modernisation of agricultural production are resulting in a search for new ways of organising labour and in the development of new working relationships between men. In 1964 the first Party Congress recommended 'strengthening mutual aid between the peasants' and 'developing cooperative production wherever conditions are most favourable to it'. The Guinean Workers' Union (UNTG), which is responsible for production in the liberated areas, has made an effort to supply the peasants with seeds on a collective basis. And the concessions abandoned by the Portuguese colonists have been put in the hands of development committees.

Thus the bases of a new economic organisation have been laid – a more democratic organisation destined to take the place of economic domination by the Portuguese.

Mozambique or The Threat of White Power

The Origins of the Struggle and the FRELIMO

The war in Mozambique is a guerilla war, with all the characteristics of guerilla warfare. The Front controls the countryside and the villages in the north. The Portuguese retain possession of the larger population centres and move along the roads and tracks in armed convoys.*

The armed struggle in Mozambique began later than in Angola or Guinea Bissao, and it has been complicated considerably both by tribal structures and by the many important West European, South African and Rhodesian economic interests which have a footing in the country.

The appeal for a general uprising was made on 25 September 1964. But Mozambique had been in a state of conflict for a long time before that, and persecutions, massacres of partisans, and clandestine movements had been common for a number of years.

It is difficult to pinpoint the exact moment at which the people can be said to have become conscious of its exploitation. In Mozambique, as in Angola, literary movements and cultural associations were the first to express the discontents of a population under colonial rule. In the twenties the few Africans who had learned to read and write grouped themselves around a number of poets in Beira and Lourenço Marques; here too, poetry served as a vehicle of protest.

Before the coming of fascism in Portugal, various legal organisations had appeared proclaiming their opposition to the regime and demanding equality for the Africans. Amongst these was the *Grémio Africano* (African Guild), which published a newspaper called *O Brado Africano (The African Cry)*.

Salazarism put an end to the possibility of fighting colonialism within the law. Clandestine organisations were then formed, often giving birth to semi-legal organisations such as the African Association and the Central Association of the Negroes of Mozambique, both of which unfortunately developed along racialist lines – one being for mulattoes, the other for blacks. In one of the last interviews he gave, a week before his assassination, Eduardo Mondlane explained: 'We began to sense that if we could rally the youth in some form of organisation we might begin some nucleus that would be meaningful politically. This was when the first nucleus of students was established, in 1949.'*

In 1948, following an uprising in Lourenço Marques, several hundred Africans were deported to São Tomé. Repression followed rebellion for a number of years. And in 1956 forty-nine workers were shot down during a dock-strike.

Massacre in Mueda

At this time, Rhodesia was still under the British mandate and therefore relatively democratic compared with the Portuguese colonies, and often served as a refuge for Mozambican nationalists who were wanted by the PIDE. The UDENAMO or National Democratic Union of Mozambique was formed in Salisbury, while others went into exile in Tanganyika – now Tanzania – where they formed the Mozambique African National Union or MANU. Strongly influenced by the situation in Tanganyika, which seemed well on the way to achieving independence, delegates of the MANU then decided to enter into negotiations with the Portuguese authorities. Several delegations, led by Faustino Vanomba, Tiago Mula, Simão Mchusa and Modesta, tried to lay the Mozambican people's demand for independence before the administrator of Mueda. Since these delegations were not even received by the Portuguese authorities, the two existing political organisations, the MANU and the UDENAMO, formed a united delegation led by Vanomba and Kibiriti. A meeting was fixed for 16 June 1960 when the governor of the Cabo Delgado district was to receive the petitioners in person and address the people. The day began in an atmosphere of popular rejoicing – it ended in the deliberate massacre of at least a thousand Africans. 'I have spoken with your comrades,' said the governor. 'Are there any amongst you who support their petition?' Hundreds of hands were raised. A dozen of those who had raised their hands were singled out at random to frighten the rest, and led away by the police; then the two delegates were handcuffed in full view of the people. The latter surged forward and the governor gave the order to open fire.

The delegates and their supporters who had survived the massacre were all imprisoned. Two weeks later a 'commission of inquiry' was set up, consisting entirely of whites. But it was too late. The people of Mozambique had learned their lesson at Mueda; believing that they had been called upon to discuss the possibility of independence publicly, they had discovered to their cost what were the colonial authorities' real intentions. The day of 16 June is no longer a day of mourning in Mozambique – it now commemorates the reaffirmation of the struggle against the Portuguese.

Three years later, in 1963, there were uprisings in the sugar-cane plantations in the Inhambane region, and these too were met with bloody reprisals. In 1963 a dock strike resulted in arrests and deaths amongst the dockers.

Meanwhile many patriots had left the country and were pursuing the struggle abroad. An important turning point was reached in June 1962 when the three political organisations – MANU, UDENAMO and UNAMI (African Union of Independent Mozambique) – joined forces to form the FRELIMO. Three months later, at the congress of 25 September 1962, Professor Eduardo Mondlane was elected president of the front. Uria Simango was named vice-president and Marcelino Dos Santos secretary for foreign relations.

The rest of 1962 and the following year were devoted to preparations for the armed struggle. The FRELIMO began to train political and military cadres to prepare the way for the insurrection. The programme of the 1962 congress consisted of four chief items:

– Setting up a political organisation inside Mozambique.
– Preparing for the armed struggle.
– Mounting propaganda campaigns against Portugal abroad.
– Starting a programme of primary, secondary and technical education and sending students to foreign universities.

This four-point programme has now been practically fulfilled. In the two years from 1962 to 1964, the FRELIMO's militants organised the struggle in the countryside, making use of the few organisations already in existence, such as agricultural cooperatives and economic and trading organisations. This political groundwork was carried out on a clearly national basis. The FRELIMO had to solve problems which were peculiar to Mozambique, and which at that time were not concerned with tribal conflicts and rivalries alone, but with regional differences as well. The three movements which had gone to make up the FRELIMO were established in three separate regions and some effort was required to make the merger effective in these areas. There was no discrimination against whites who wished to join the movement.

The preparations needed for the war were substantial. In this respect the FRELIMO had to start from scratch. However, Algeria, having just achieved its own independence, agreed to train men and set up a special programme for Mozambique. The first group left at the end of 1962. A corps returned at the end of 1963 to train others on the spot. By June 1964, 200 men were trained and reasonably well equipped.

For the propaganda campaign against the Portuguese government, offices were opened in Dar es Salaam, Cairo, Algiers and in New York, with a special eye on the UN.

Finally the education programme has already achieved some results. In 1962 only fifteen young Mozambicans were at university. Now 150 Mozambican students are at universities around the world, thanks to scholarships given to the FRELIMO by foreign countries. And more than 20,000 children are at school in the liberated province of Cabo Delgado.

'The General Armed Insurrection of the Mozambican People'

In July 1964 the Central Committee of the FRELIMO met in order to hear for the last time the arguments for and against an armed struggle, and to take the supreme decision of declaring 'the general armed insurrection of the Mozambican people against Portuguese colonialism'. The declaration was officially made on 25 September 1964. Today this date has become the occasion for a day of growing international demonstrations of solidarity with the people of Mozambique.

Military activities began on a small scale in the provinces of Niassa, Tete, Zambézia and Cabo Delgado. In the provinces of Zambézia and Tete, the combatants had to withdraw after six months. The war was continued, however, in the provinces of Niassa and Cabo Delgado. Today, almost

the whole of Cabo Delgado and two-thirds of Niassa –
nearly 150,000 square kilometres inhabited by about 800,000
people – are in the hands of the FRELIMO, except the
towns. In the province of Niassa, all the villages are cut off
including the capital, Vila Cabral.

In 1967, military operations were given a new impetus as
the FRELIMO began to undertake combined operations
with infantry and artillery units. The Portuguese bases of
Nacatara, Maniamba, Sipaki, Nambude and Nova Coimbra
were attacked and quantities of equipment were captured.

The opening of the Tete Front in March 1968 was the
most important event in the fourth year of the struggle in
Mozambique. This front was of considerable strategic importance since military operations could now be extended
into the centre of the country and spread out towards the
south and the northern centre. The FRELIMO's control
over this third zone of activity, however, is not nearly so
extensive as in the regions of Niassa and Cabo Delgado.

In addition, the concentration of Portuguese military
strength is much higher in Tete than elsewhere because of
the construction of the giant Cabora Bassa dam, which is
being built, essentially, to provide electricity for South
Africa. From 1964, when the FRELIMO's armed forces
went into action in the Niassa and Cabo Delgado districts,
Portugal concentrated her troops between Nacala on the
coast and Mandimba on the frontier with Malawi, in order
to contain the FRELIMO behind this line. In fact the line
was broken in 1965. Today one aspect of the Cabora Bassa
project has become clear – if Portugal succeeds in finishing
the dam, she will at the same time succeed in blocking the
FRELIMO's progress towards the south, and prevent the
FRELIMO's forces from joining up with the other liberation movements in South Africa and Rhodesia.

In April 1968 a military commission from the OAU
visited the liberated regions of Mozambique and found
them cleared of the Portuguese presence.

In July 1968 the FRELIMO was able to hold its Second

Congress in the province of Niassa, within Mozambique itself. The discussions, which some people had come a very long way to take part in, lasted six days.

On 3 February 1969, Eduardo Mondlane was assassinated in Dar es Salaam, by a bomb hidden inside a book.* In May the Central Committee of the FRELIMO elected the commander-in-chief of the Armed Forces, Samora Machel, and Marcelino Dos Santos as acting president and vice-president in charge of foreign affairs respectively.

While the FRELIMO inevitably experienced a crisis in 1969, after the death of Eduardo Mondlane, today this crisis seems to be over. Marcelino Dos Santos said recently:

> We have consolidated the structure of our politico-military and administrative power in the liberated zones with significant increases in agricultural production, fishing and local crafts; we have increased the number of schools and teachers and improved their quality at the same time; we have developed the health services and trained a large number of medical workers and nurses. Today each combat unit has a medical orderly travelling with it. The development of our combatants' political conscience should also be underlined, for today more than ever we are convinced that the basis of our victory resides largely in the constant elevation and political training of our combatants, our cadres, and generally speaking of our people.*

National Reconstruction

Today, with its large liberated zones, Mozambique too is faced with the mammoth problem of providing subsistence for its people and practically reconstructing the national economy. When they retreat in the face of the national liberation army's troops, the Portuguese leave a vacuum behind them. The few remaining vestiges of local administration disappear. The schools, hospitals and religious missions run by the Portuguese have to be closed. The

Portuguese traders leave the region, and the commercial companies close their doors. In addition, the villagers often have to leave their villages in order to escape from air raids, and establish themselves in the depths of the forest. In short, the basic infrastructure which has existed for decades is swept away in a few days. It has to be replaced – and on a new and different basis.

In the provinces of Niassa and Cabo Delgado, and in certain areas of the province of Tete, there are some million Mozambicans who rely on the FRELIMO for everything – schools, clinics, hospitals, and work.

As from 1966 the Central Committee of the FRELIMO laid emphasis on the need for educating the masses, and proclaimed two important principles:

– Only education can bring total liberation.
– Education is as important in the struggle as the battle-front itself.

Thus education in the liberated zones was not only a question of teaching pure and simple, but also had to be present in every branch of revolutionary activity. There was an urgent need to train cadres and politicised militants. The educational system adopted by the leaders of the FRELIMO is based on the principle that, firstly, the individuals to be educated should be chosen for their civic qualities and their political behaviour and, secondly, there is a need for educated leaders, but also for an educated people. New text-books have been written, often by the teachers themselves. They are used in the schools, together with the basic political texts of the FRELIMO. The former teachers of the colonial regime are forced either to adapt to a new form of teaching or to leave. New teachers are trained, and the course for primary teachers lasts six months. Foreign teachers are sometimes accepted.

The results already achieved are remarkable. In the province of Niassa, where the work of national reconstruction is furthest advanced, there were only three teachers when the Portuguese left in 1964. In January 1970 there were 120 schools and 191 teachers educating 12,000 pupils. The FRELIMO also seems to have attacked the problem of female emancipation. Parents are encouraged to send their daughters to school, even though the children at times have to spend the night out of doors in bomb shelters. Secondary education does not yet exist in free Mozambique. However, a secondary school for Mozambican pupils has been founded in Tanzania.

A health campaign is under way on several fronts. The first step was to create first aid posts to deal with urgent cases, and field hospitals in accessible places. Thus, the field hospital of Cabo Delgado, donated by the Italian province of Reggio Emilia, for instance, was able to treat about 3,500 people in the year 1968-9. There were several field hospitals functioning in Niassa in 1970. A great effort has also been made in preventive medicine. Vaccination campaigns preceded by efforts to educate the masses have had some promising results. Finally, nurses and medical orderlies are being trained as quickly as possible.

It is in the economic field, however, that the work of reconstruction can be most clearly seen. Mozambique's resources are essentially agricultural and mineral. In agriculture, they had been made to serve the needs of Portugal, and crops such as cotton, oil palms and tobacco were grown chiefly for export. The FRELIMO had two options – either it could continue this type of production in liberated zones and try to export it profitably, using the revenue to buy the most urgently needed goods; or it could attempt to transform the economy completely and turn to a type of agriculture which could first feed the liberated peoples and the guerillas as in Guinea. It was this second path which was chosen. The liberated zones of Mozambique now produce maize, corn, manioc, haricot beans, potatoes and rice for local consumption; and copra, rye, tobacco, castor oil seeds, ground-nuts, sesame seeds, cashew nuts, and rubber for export since 1966. An early buyer of free Mozambique pro-

duce was Egypt. Cotton weaving and soap manufacture has
begun. 'People's shops' have been opened for the exchange
of goods, and fishermen's cooperatives have been formed to
provide their men with equipment and distribute their
produce.

Agricultural production is organised on three levels – in
the military camps, where the soldiers cultivate the land
according to their needs; in the 'national camps' which exist
in each district, where the land is cultivated on a rota by
men from the villages and the produce is sent directly to
the FRELIMO, which redistributes it to the people, to the
military camps and sales organisations; and finally in
'people's camps', where the inhabitants decide what they
will produce according to their tastes, their needs, and the
facilities available. This form of production has yet to fulfil
the needs of liberated areas. However, each year would
seem to bring an improvement.

FOUR

Portugal, the Servant of Great Powers

Selling the Colonies

Needing substantial financial aid to pursue its colonial wars, the Portuguese government launched an appeal to the countries of the West. But it has paid a high price for this support, and this price has been a gradual loss of sovereignty in Africa. Angola and Mozambique are now wide open to an influx of foreign capital, and Portugal increasingly does no more than serve the interests of the great powers.

The Overseas Territories are not closed to foreign capital, and the latter will be placed there in large quantities, because private capital is attracted above all by the stability and honesty of the administration, which in practical terms means security for investments. And we are not speaking of our own plans for development in these territories, which are showing quite remarkable results.

Such were the intentions of the Portuguese government as revealed by Salazar in 1963. In 1965 a law was passed which modified and completed the previous system. In particular, this law permitted the creation of companies in which foreign organisations held a majority interest, 'providing their actions are in conformity with the country's plans for economic development'. It was also stipulated that foreign investors could freely transfer the interest, dividends and bonuses which they received from this capital, and even transfer the capital itself to their home countries without any limit. The terms were obviously attractive, and the United States, Great Britain, France, the Netherlands, Belgium, and, above all, West Germany and South Africa, were quick to take an interest.

This move by the Salazar government was not an entirely new departure, but served to accentuate an already existing state of affairs. The economic powers present in Angola and Mozambique before and since the beginning of the armed struggle in 1961 are as follows.

In Angola, all the resources of the subsoil are exploited by foreign companies. Let us briefly list the main organisations concerned. The Diamang – which mines diamonds – is an offshoot of the Anglo-American Diamond Corporation Ltd., in which the De Beers group, the Morgan Bank and the Société Générale de Belgique also have an interest. This company is granted exemption from taxes and customs duty on its imports of machinery and exports of diamonds, and its concessions cover almost half of the country. The Angola government owns 15 per cent of the basic capital.

Between 1967 and 1969 the output of the Diamang rose by 55 per cent, from 1,300,000 carats in 1967 to 1,667,000 carats in 1968 to 2,021,000 carats in 1969, which was an all-time production record. Diamond exports, however, rose more slowly from 1,300,000 carats in 1967 to 1,500,000 carats in 1968, but the export value rose from 1,204 million to 1,361 million escudos.

During 1969 the Portuguese Government granted four new diamond concessions in Angola. These were: (*1*) the Oestiediam–Companhia de Diamantes Oeste de Angola, SARL with a capital of 15 million escudos and which has the financial and technical backing of the Diamond Distributors, Inc., of New York; (2) Diversa–International de Explorações de Diamantes, SARL which is backed by Diversa, Inc., a United States company; (3) Companhia

Ultramarina de Diamantes, SARL (DIAMUL) which also has United States support; and (4) Companhia Nacional de Diamantes, SARL (DINACO), which is owned by the Anchor Diamond Corporation Ltd, a South African Company.

Petroleum is exploited by Lobito Fuel Oil, which is 70 per cent owned by the Belgian company Petrofina. In Cabinda the chief producer is the Cabinda Gulf Oil Company, a wholly owned subsidiary of the United States Gulf Oil Corporation, and the Petrangol-Angol group which is largely owned by Belgian and Portuguese interests. Operating in association with Petrangol-Angol was the Compagnie Française des Pétroles of France and Texaco. In April 1972 the Argo Petroleum Corporation of Los Angeles obtained five concessions covering 3·1 million acres, of which four, onshore and offshore in Southern Angola, included production rights up to thirty years.

Contrary to expectations, total crude petroleum production in 1968, at 749,514 tons, was lower than preliminary estimates. Out of the total production, 558,979 tons were from Petrangol-Angol and 190,535 tons from the Cabinda Gulf Oil Company. During 1968, the Luanda refinery processed 663,702 tons of crude petroleum, of which 168,702 tons were imported. Exports of fuel oil amounted to 48,100 tons valued at 15·8 million escudos, compared with 58,298 tons valued at 29·8 million escudos in 1967. Exports of crude petroleum in 1969 amounted to more than 400 million escudos. In 1969, in addition to a request by Petrangol-Angol for a new concession area, there were seventeen applications for concessions from other companies pending a decision by the Portuguese Government.

Manganese is entirely controlled by the German company of Louise A. Therese Berman. Aluminium is exploited by Aluminio Portugues, which is a cover for the French Pechiney company. Bauxite is worked by the Dutch company of Billiton Maatschappij. Iron ore is extracted by the Companhia Mineira de Lobito – a consortium in which Krupps of Essen (Germany) have the majority interest, together with Gregg-Europe (Belgium), Hojgaard and Schultz (Denmark), and Pirelli and the Venice Dockyards (Italy). The Germans now hold the majority interest in the Angolan iron industry. In 1963 46 per cent of the total investment in Angolan industry was German. Krupp and Berman control 7 per cent of the total iron ore reserves in Angola and 82·7 per cent of the iron ore currently exported. It is easy to see why, today, West Germany is the Portuguese regime's chief means of support.

Of the country's coffee, 80 per cent is handled by the Companhia Agricola de Angola, which belongs to the French Rallet bank. Cotton goes to concessionary firms who buy at fixed prices; the biggest are the Société Générale de Belgique, represented by the Companhia Geral de Algodoes, the Banque Belge d'Afrique and the Angolan Cotton Company.

In Mozambique the situation is more or less the same. It is estimated that 80 per cent of investments are made by international groups. Three large companies have controlled two-thirds of the economy since 1900. These are the Mozambique Company, based on British, German and South African capital; the Niassa Company, with British capital; and the Zambézia Company, with British, German, French and South African capital.

Guinea Bissao has not been so systematically exploited by foreign companies because it is not of great economic interest to them. The Guinean economy is basically in the hands of the Portuguese monopoly, the Companhia União Fabril (CUF) and the Portuguese National Overseas Bank. The CUF has associated interests with firms in West Germany, France and the United States. In 1962 it signed a contract with the Société Française d'Etudes et de Financements Industriels for the erection of workshops in Guinea. All banking activities in Guinea are centralised in the Banco Nacional Ultramarino. Amongst its associates are the Crédit Franco-Portugais, the Comptoir National d'Escompte de Paris, the Midland Bank Executor and Trust Company, the Westminster Bank Ltd., and the Banco Hispano-Americano. Oil prospecting in Guinea Bissao is entirely in the hands of Esso Exploration Guinea Inc., whose head office is in the United States. A contract signed in March 1968 gives the company the right to prospect for oil and exploit it on its own account for a period of forty-five years, throughout the entire territory of Guinea. The Standard Oil Company and Esso can also undertake prospecting for and exploitation of any other mineral.

The infiltration of foreign capital is constantly growing. In Angola the penetration of German companies such as Krupp and the Deutsche Bank is increasing, while in Mozambique more and more concessions are being given for oil prospecting. The Gulf Oil Company, Clark Oil, Hunt International and a Franco-South African consortium consisting of Anglo-American on the South African side and SNP-Aquitaine and Erap-Elf on the French side are all prospecting for what promises to become an oil boom of some importance.

The French Atomic Energy Commission now buys Mozambique's entire production of radioactive ore, and France is also active in prospecting. Air Liquide has invested 40 million francs in Angola; the Compagnie Générale des Petroles d'Aquitaine and the Bureau de Recherches Géologiques et Minières are prospecting the subsoil in Angola and Mozambique. Valery Giscard d'Estaing's 'safari' in Angola in 1969 was no doubt chiefly intended to ensure that France would have a share of Angolan oil, if supplies from Algeria were to dry up for one reason or another.

It is, therefore, understandable that certain financial circles are leading a campaign in favour of the Portuguese policy in Africa. And it is a fact that industry, and particularly those parts of it concerned with mining and oil extraction, tend to develop just as national liberation movements are beginning to show their strength. This was certainly the case in Algeria, where the exploitation of the country's oil resources and the Constantine plan were begun after the outbreak of war. Perhaps it represents an attempt by the colonial regime to demonstrate to foreign powers that the colony should be maintained as it is.

Unfortunately, however, this sudden revival of the economy does not generally stem from any serious plans for the country's development. It is always the production of raw materials destined purely for export which tends to shoot up. There is never any sign of an enterprise being started in the interests of the colonial country itself, such as an important and sensibly based manufacturing industry instead of the customary small textile factories, conservation plants, cement works and breweries. In agriculture monocultivation for export continues to be the rule, in spite of the needs of the population and the extreme state of dependence which this type of production imposes on the country.

But just as the Constantine plan did not prevent Algeria from gaining her independence, so the Africans of Angola and Mozambique will undoubtedly not allow any illusions about the nature of current developments to dissuade them from their aims. And it seems reasonable to suppose that far from putting an end to the claims for national independence, the new investments, the dam-building, the improvement of roads, and the whole of the new Portuguese development plan, will merely serve to prove to the people of Angola and Mozambique that the struggle pays dividends.

'Marry an African'

The idea of populating the 'overseas provinces' dates back before the last ten years, having appeared little by little in the thinking of the Salazar regime. Previously, the nineteenth-century style exploitation of the colonies had not called for a substantial European population. The development of their mineral and vegetable resources merely required an abundance of native labour directed by a handful of whites, together with sufficient troops to keep order, quartered in garrisons. The big commercial enterprises were managed by Europeans, while small-scale trading was left either to minorities – Indians, Lebanese and Greeks – or to the few 'assimilated' natives who often supported the regime.

England and Belgium had taken this system further by creating predominantly native forces to keep order, commanded by European officers.

The coming of Salazarism brought about a change. First of all, it had become necessary, since 1885, to maintain some kind of presence in the colonies if they were to be protected from take-over ... by rival colonial powers.

In addition, the Salazar regime was particularly eager to justify the Portuguese presence in Africa, to create the image of a global, multiracial Portugal, helping its African sister to maintain the liberty and equality of all her citizens. But the image had to be supported by actions, and thus Portuguese emigration to the colonies was started.

At the same time, Portugal's economic and social development was hardly favourable to such an expansion. For a colony to be populated from the outside, certain conditions must exist in the colonising country. For example, a substantial growth in the population accompanied by a lack of employment at home. Now Portugal has never met these two conditions simultaneously. There has never been a galloping increase in the birth-rate, and with 8 million inhabitants in 1970 Portugal is one of the least populated countries in Europe, considering its size. There has on the other hand been an appreciable lack of economic development, which the Salazar regime was unable to combat, and the situation has worsened during the past few years.

In 1900, there were 9,000 Portuguese settlers in Angola,

a bare 1,500 in Mozambique and a negligible number in Guinea. Under the Salazar regime, the Portuguese population were constantly urged to settle in the colonies. In fact, as the poverty of the Portuguese masses increases, the workers show an increasing tendency to emigrate elsewhere. Poverty is the direct result of the political and economic concepts of Salazar and his successor, which have prevented any large-scale industrialisation and any economic development along modern lines. If Salazar or Caetano wanted to develop Portugal today, they would have to pay the price in one way or another. The Portuguese socialist leader in exile, Mario Soares asked: 'What would this price be? A reform of the country's internal structure which would make Portuguese industry and agriculture competitive; the abandoning of the disastrous experiment of corporative government; and a return to freedom for the trade unions.'*

In order to prevent the workers from emigrating to the United States, France and West Germany – 150,000 Portuguese left the country in 1970 – the government would have had to deal with the basic reason for this exodus – the poverty at home. In order to convince them that they should settle in the colonies rather than elsewhere, it would have had to make sure that they could live there in peace and comfort. Neither of these conditions were fulfilled. The economy of the Portuguese colonies was entirely tied up in the hands of monopolistic Portuguese and international capitalists, and left little opportunity for individuals to get rich. Moreover the Portuguese army is now no longer able to guarantee the complete safety of the whites, at least over large areas, or at the cost of restrictions on their freedom of movement within each country. The Salazar regime offered numerous subsidies to those who were prepared to settle in Angola or Mozambique. And there was even a special premium for every Portuguese who would marry an African woman – a somewhat ironic detail in the context of a soi-disant non-racialist system.

In fact, despite the wishes of his government, the Portuguese peasant prefers to emigrate to the highly industrialised countries. The Paris weekly *L'Express* of 2 April 1972 remarked that in the last ten years one-third of Portugal's active population have chosen the way of exile and that there were less Portuguese settlers in the African colonies than Portuguese immigrants in France alone. From 1951 to 1960, out of a total of 600,000 emigrants, only a fifth went to Africa. Emigration to the colonies grew continuously up to 1959. Between 1960 and 1963 it was stopped by the fear of war; it began again tentatively in 1964-5, then decreased again in 1966.

In 1970, the total number of Portuguese in the colonies was distributed as follows: approximately 20,000 in Guinea Bissao, almost all of them soldiers and some 5,000 in Cape Verde; 400,000 in Angola, including the military (estimated at 70,000 men) and nearly 3,000 in São Tomé and Príncipe; 210,000 in Mozambique, again including the white armed forces numbering 60,000.

In order for the colony to become a colonial settlement, like Algeria, under the French, a far greater number of Europeans would be needed. But nowhere do they amount to more than 5 per cent of the population. In addition, the settlers show an increasing tendency to withdraw into the towns, and prefer speculation to working on the land. One consequence of this attempt to establish a colonial settlement was not perhaps foreseen in the original policy – the European settlers are now involved in a political separatist movement which is passing from a national to an international level; for there can be no doubt that in order to maintain their position, the European minority will have to call upon emigrants from other European countries, and particularly call on the military support of Pretoria and Salisbury. Agostinho Neto writes:

It is obvious that the settlers are not planning to give up their property, not only because their holdings are vast, but also because of the easy exploitation of man-power from among the Angolan people, who are forced to work for almost nothing. Some are even thinking of seceding from Portugal so as to rule the country them-selves, as happened in Rhodesia....

The settlers are our most dangerous enemies, because they are the most bellicose; they hate the Angolan popu-lation and are, in turn, hated by it....

In [the north] there are many German farmers who left the German Democratic Republic at the time of the liberation of that country.*

Cabora Bassa

By far the greatest threat today to the liberation move-ments in the Overseas Territories, and in particular to the FRELIMO in Mozambique, is the relatively recent pro-ject of the Cabora Bassa dam on the Zambezi in the pro-vince of Tete. Because of its frontiers with Malawi, Zambia and Rhodesia, this province is of great strategic import-ance. It lies in the centre of the colony and is crossed by a number of important lines of communication, amongst which is the road from Salisbury (in Rhodesia) to Blantyre (in Malawi). The region is one of the richest in Mozam-bique, both in agriculture, stock-raising and the resources of the subsoil. The site of the Cabora Bassa dam lies where the three territories of Zambia, Malawi and Rhodesia meet and where the Zambezi, which enters Mozambique at 1,000 ft., drops 400 ft. in a gorge 60 miles long – 300 miles away from its outlet on the Indian Ocean.

Let us first of all deal with the technical aspect of the project. The dam, which will be the largest in Africa – twice the size of the Kariba and 70 per cent bigger than the Aswan dam in Egypt – will create an artificial lake of 2,700 square kilometres, nearly 230 kilometres long and with an estimated capacity of 65 million cubic metres. The lake will be able to feed a hydro-electric generating station with an annual production of 17 million kilowatt-hours and a power of 3,600 megawatts. It will be the fourth largest generating station in the world, and the turbines and generators designed for the generating plant will be the largest ever used in the West. The turbines will be supplied by the firms of Volth and Siemens, the generators by Siemens and Alsthom. Because of the enormous distance between Cabora Bassa and Johannesburg, the power will be carried over a distance of nearly 1,400 kilometres – 7,000 pylons at 400-metre intervals – and this is another world record, since the longest high-tension line existing at present, the Pacific Intertie, is only 1,350 kilometres long. The current will be carried at 1,066,000 volts. Again, this will be the highest voltage used for carrying power anywhere in the world, and is substantially above that of the Pacific Intertie at 800,000 volts. The current will leave a distribution centre belonging to the Compagnie Générale d'Entreprise Electrique, and be carried to a transformer station. There the alternating current will be turned into direct current by the Thyristor and Solid State systems of Siemens and AEG. On arriving at its destination, the direct current will be turned back into alternating current at 275,000 volts in the Apollo Centre in Johannesburg, again using the Thyristor and Solid State systems. Construction work on the first phase began in October 1969, to be finished before March 1975.

This project will be carried out by and for other people than the Africans. Finance is to be provided by export loans from France, Germany and South Africa, and private European capital raised through the Bank of Paris and the Netherlands, whose board of directors was recently joined by the famous South African banker Oppenheimer. Out of the total cost, France is to carry 72 million dollars, Portugal 35 million, and the remainder will be borne by South Africa.

In September 1969, the Portuguese Government awarded the contract for the construction of the Cabora Bassa dam to Zamco-Zambezi Consortium Hidroelectrico, the consortium headed by South African interests. Since Zamco was first organised, one of the original companies, Allmänna Svenska Elektriska Aktiebolaget (ASEA) has withdrawn and eight new companies have been included, of which six are French, one is Italian and one is Portuguese.

The new Zamco consortium is composed of the following companies, marked with an asterisk in the case of those represented in the original consortium.

1. Allgemeine Elektricitats-Gesellschaft AEG-Telefunken – Germany*
2. Brown Boveri and Cie – Germany*
3. Compagnie Générale d'Entreprises Electriques (CGEE – Cogelex) – France*
4. Entreprise Fougerolle-Limousin – France
5. Hochtief Aktiengesellschaft – Germany*
6. J. M. Voith Gmbh – Germany*
7. LTA Ltd – Johannesburg – South Africa*
8. Siemens Aktiengesellschaft – Germany*
9. Shaft Sinkers (Proprietary) Ltd. – South Africa*
10. Sociedades Reunidas de Fabricações Metálicas – Sorefame, SARL – Portugal
11. Società Anonima Elettrificazione, SpA – Italy
12. Société Générale de Constructions Electriques et Mécaniques Alshtom – France*
13. Compagnie de Constructions Internationales – France*
14. Société des Grands Travaux de Marseille – France
15. Société Générale d'Entreprises – France
16. Société Française d'Entreprises de Dragages et de Travaux Publics – France
17. Compagnie Industrielle de Travaux – France
18. Entreprises Campenon-Bernard – France

Its composition was altered when, in May 1971, it was announced that the US Government had refused to grant credits to the General Electric Company, which had joined the Consortium. Earlier, the Italian Government had told SAE (*Società Anonima Elettrificazione*) it could not use in the Cabora Bassa project the credits it had originally been granted for this purpose, because of risks involved. The Italian Government acted following talks with President Kaunda.* But in October 1971, it was learned that still another German firm, 'Messrs. Pohlig-Heckel-Bleichert', had been enrolled to build two huge cranes that would cover every spot of the construction.

The economic importance of the project is considerable. First of all, the area in which the dam is being built is relatively rich in natural resources. Investigations undertaken by the Portuguese government over the past few years have revealed the existence of a number of minerals, including coal, copper, fluor, manganese, beryllium, corundum, chromium, graphite, magnetite, nickel, titanium and aluminium. The iron is only beginning to be exploited, but it is estimated that it could bring in £25 million sterling when exported. Then there is the electricity which will be produced from the dam. Half of this will be bought by South Africa, who will use it chiefly in the mines of the Transvaal. All the riches of the subsoil in the region can be exploited at a very low outlay.

The construction of the dam will also permit the intensive cultivation of a further 1·5 million hectares of land, out of which 200,000 will be devoted to reafforestation and tropical plantations. The Portuguese settlers have always shown a preference for this region, and they already own a large proportion of its cultivable land. The Portuguese regime is carrying out a campaign for the rapid settlement of about a million whites – Portuguese, South Africans and Rhodesians.

To house these newcomers a new town is projected, the town of Cabora Bassa, in the Songo region. The initial work will be carried out by the Portuguese government. The first houses and schools were to be completed in June 1970; the first families were to arrive in December 1970. According to a publicity brochure issued by the Portuguese in West Germany:

The town of Cabora Bassa lies at an altitude of 930 metres. The climate is good for Europeans. The area offers considerable facilities for fishing, hunting etc. Water supplies are more than adequate and communications with the outside world – via Songo airport – are excellent.*

Circulars are being distributed to Portuguese workers in Germany and France urging them to go and settle in Mozambique. If Portugal seems prepared to lose the 7 to 8 million contos she receives annually from Portuguese workers abroad – which is almost as much as the annual deficit in the Portuguese trade balance – it is because the Cabora Bassa project, although extremely expensive initially, promises to be extremely profitable in the near future.

According to the Lisbon *Diario de Noticias* (December 1969):

The progress constituted by the construction of the Cabora Bassa dam will not only make it possible to put an end to the guerilla activities which have been going on in the north of Mozambique for the past five years, but also to settle a million Portuguese in the Zambezi valley – development which will be of the greatest importance not only for the future of Mozambique, but also for the whole of southern Africa.

Thus the Cabora Bassa project is clearly the cornerstone of Portuguese colonial policy today.

The essential factor in this programme is of course the construction of the dam, and this is constantly threatened by the armed forces of the FRELIMO. Here again, Portuguese policy has been caught in its own contradictions. More than 20,000 Africans have already been displaced from their land so that the dam can be built, and a good number of them have certainly gone to join the revolutionary front in the province of Tete. South Africa keeps troops in Mozambique in order to guard the construction work. Once the dam is built it will block the FRELIMO's progress to the south. The intention is clearly to increase the hold of South Africa on Mozambique. The Cabora Bassa dam will turn all southern Africa's geopolitical perspectives upside down. According to the *Stuttgarter Zeitung*, the Tete region could become an 'African Ruhr'. The dam is only part of an electrical energy network linking the three white governments of the Pretoria–Salisbury –Lisbon axis. According to the *Johannesburg Star*, this network constitutes the first step towards 'the establishment of an economic community in southern Africa' in which South Africa herself will play a decisive role. It is by no means unlikely that a strong white minority may one day take the reins of power in Mozambique, and there will then be a Salisbury–Pretoria–Lourenço Marques axis, which will be all to the advantage of Pretoria. The South African Union is thus defending not only its financial interests, but also its political interests, as they were expressed by the Portuguese Foreign Minister:

> After an examination of their mutual interests, the two signatories have arrived at a satisfactory result. This has demonstrated once more the profound agreement of interests of all the countries of Central Africa, the last bastion of Western civilisation on a continent torn by troubles and tragedies.*

Cunene

South Africa and Portugal found a common interest, similar to that of Cabora Bassa, in Angola's Cunene hydrographic and electric scheme. Although less known than the Cabora Bassa project, this scheme is even more ambitious (its cost is estimated at £250 million, as against £171 million for Cabora Bassa) and is based on the Cunene river which originates at Nova Lisboa, on the limits of the zone of heavy and regular rains in Western Angola. The Cunene then flows for some 1,000 kms. almost parallel to the coast to end towards the desert areas of Namibia.

This scheme, prepared by Pretoria in 1962, was agreed between South Africa and Portugal on 21 January 1969, and would consist of a series of hydro-electric dams:

Gove	– 25	MW	Chissola	– 6,5	MW
Jamba-Ia-Oma	– 39	MW	Gungué	– 4	MW
Chivondua	– 15	MW	Lacundo	– 6,5	MW
Jamba-Ia-Mina	– 81,5	MW	Cabundi	– 14,5	MW
Matundo	– 50	MW	Catembulo	– 5	MW
Total	 210,5	MW	Total	 36,5	MW

Grand Total 247 MW

A dam at Gove, to create an artificial lake of 2,574 cubic metres, some 100 kms. from the industrial town of Nova Lisboa, on the upper Cunene, was initiated in January 1969. The hydro-electric station here would augment the power of the Matala electric station, which powers the Cassinga mines exploited by Krupp with the assistance of a huge loan of the Inter-American Capital Corporation. The local semi-nomad population of 37,000 would be installed in *aldeamentos* elsewhere and 6,000 white families would be settled around the Gove station, which would also provide 100 million gallons of water per day to South African controlled Ovamboland.

The entire Cunene project, which would allow the irrigation of some 500,000 hectares would ultimately cost 437 million rand, 50 per cent of which would be provided by Pretoria. As the Portuguese have been scared by the advance of MPLA elements along the Kuando river and were hesitant, South Africa advanced the sum of 5.8 million to initiate the Gove project.

White Power

Thus a new political project would seem to be under way, whereby power will simply be transferred to the white settlers. *Fraternidade* is dead, if indeed it ever existed. For the African, the Portuguese colonist is a foreigner, to be treated according to which camp he is in. For the small settler, the African is a threat. For the big colonialists he is a source of labour for their increasingly independent capitalist projects. In Luanda, Benguela, Beira and Lourenço Marques, there now exist groups of Portuguese mixed with other white elements who are consciously racist – their racism being founded on colour and social class – and who intend to stay that way. Their standards are so low that they even take the jobs of African manual workers. The recent formation of groups of armed settlers, both official and clandestine, is a significant development. The new Portuguese leaders know that the colonies have already escaped from Lisbon's control.

Together with the increasing amount of foreign investment in Angola and Mozambique, a new variant of the ruling class is appearing in the form of big industrialists and financiers acting under the banner of Portuguese interests. As a result of their alliance with the international economic powers they will be able simultaneously to maintain a degree of Portuguese influence over the economic development of the colonies and persuade their partners to invest in Portugal itself. It is quite clear that this Portuguese and international class of capitalists is seeking a response from within the colonies.*

Now such a response will not be hard to find. Since the outbreak of the war, the Portuguese settlers have been drawing away from the metropolis. Some are organising themselves in armed militias and establishing contacts with the governments of South Africa and Rhodesia. Various groups in Angola and Mozambique are in fact actively preparing for an alternative form of independence – along Rhodesian lines – with a ruling class dominating the African majority by means of its capital, its police, its weapons and the certainty of being helped in this enterprise by the rest of the South African bloc. *L'Express* of

2 April 1972 asserted that the separatist movement of the whites in Angola was reaching 'unexpected proportions' and quoted a Portuguese personality back from Angola as saying: 'We are heading towards new Rhodesias'.

FIVE

NATO's Hidden Wars

VERY few people in Western Europe or North America today have any idea of the scale of Portugal's wars in Africa. There is practically no newspaper, nor radio station, nor television network which follows, to a greater or lesser degree, information about the 13 million Africans who are struggling for their independence. In December 1971, however, *The Times* reported daily and substantially on 'Italy's lead' in the European bridge tournament.

On the rare occasions when journalists and film-makers do mention the situation in the Portuguese colonies, one expression which frequently recurs is that of 'hidden wars'. But in the West, they are only hidden from public opinion. And the public's ignorance is by no means shared by general staff officers in business circles, the armaments industry and the large banks, who follow the course of events with close interest. It is not difficult to understand why; not only do early colonial status and war provide some of them with their living, but also the potential riches of Angola and Mozambique are colossal.

The great political powers are gauging the stakes in the struggle, which is now beginning to influence world strategy. And if these problems are seldom mentioned it is because precautions are taken to keep them away from the public eye. In the meantime, industrialists and politicians from France, England, Germany, Italy, Belgium, Holland and America come and go in the southern hemisphere. Their visits are seldom 'official'; they are rarely mentioned in newspapers, questions are never asked in parliament. Blantyre airport in Malawi is one of the cross-roads of this traffic.

Although it is widely known that Portugal is governed by a fascist dictatorship, in which opponents of the regime are unjustly tried, what is not so widely known is that this country is in fact given substantial financial and military support by NATO and individually by its members. At one time, apologists of Portuguese colonialism would say that this aid does not directly concern the war effort. How-ever, as the *Financial Times* commented as early as in 1964:

> That Portugal does not need foreign loans to defend the fatherland has been stressed recently by Dr Corrêa da Oliveira [the minister of State]. But the country certainly needs very considerable foreign aid to replace her own resources diverted from economic expansion to military requirements.*

A few years later, Dr Caetano himself made the follow-ing admission:

> All the military effort overseas has been, and will go on being, supported by resources coming from the ordinary income, which, before, was largely used to cover development expenses ... Now we have to face many of these expenses with money obtained by loan.*

Thus Western European and American financial aid is indirectly supporting the colonial wars at least according to the *Financial Times* and Dr Caetano himself. Though it is difficult to judge accurately the extent of these loans, we shall nevertheless attempt to do so later on, when dealing with the relations between Portugal and each of the powers in question.

Why are the Western nations secretly, but deliberately, supporting these wars? The reason is that by virtue of its natural resources and its strategic position, southern Africa is an area of supreme importance to them. Now the Western powers, and in particular the United States, are showing an increasing dependence on the natural resources in energy and minerals of the countries of the so-called third world. These resources consist primarily of ores which are becoming increasingly hard to obtain: iron ore which, in Angola as in South Africa, has a very high iron content (60-65 per cent); manganese, which is not found in the industrialised countries; vanadium, chrome, copper, lead. And there are many others not yet statistically accounted for. South Africa supplies the Western world with 70 per cent of its gold; 95 per cent of world diamond sales are effected by the South African De Beers group; and finally there is a large quantity of fissionable materials, which are becoming increasingly important with the growth of nuclear industries.

The strategic role of this region is no less considerable than its economic potential. If current plans for development are carried out, large quantities of goods will have to pass through Angola and Mozambique, and their ports will be the natural distribution points for the ores of Katanga, Rhodesia, and Zambia. The Portuguese colonies are still the strategic key to the Cape route, which has become extremely important since the closing of the Suez Canal. And the Cape Verde archipelago is an important strategic link in communications between Europe and the south Atlantic and Latin America. Thus, if the liberation movements were to win their struggle, a whole network of very substantial interests would probably collapse. The 'strategic' argument, as we know, is always used for personal ends, and there is no doubt that the Western monopolies who are profiting from the current situation would lose a lot by the fall of Portuguese colonialism. The history of Algeria, amongst others, has demonstrated that business with newly independent colonies can, of course, be carried on – but on a new basis.

Credit must go to Professor L. Barnes* for having given the most rational description of NATO's role in Africa: 'NATO control in Africa is a top-level control concerned chiefly with strategy, ideology, the relation of African states with non-African powers, and certain financial matters, particularly currency and investment. Its over-riding objective is to ensure that the behaviour of African states is acceptable to NATO, whether or not it is accept-able, or advantageous to Africans. In practice this control can be devolved within broad limits, on agencies regarded by NATO as reliable in particular geographical areas. The France–EEC combine ... the Washington–Kinshasa–Nairobi axis ... [and] ... South Africa, to some extent on probation ... [are such agencies].'

For the Defence of the Western World

On 30 May 1962 the president of Ghana said:

Portugal's position in maintaining her colonial dic-tatorship is strongly consolidated by her membership of NATO, which gives her the arms needed to kill the innocent men, women and children of Angola. Thus, Portugal can carry on this colonial war because, basic-ally, she has the support of NATO. If this support was removed, if Portugal was excluded from the organisa-tion, her colonial domination would crumble tomorrow. Would it not be worthy of the NATO powers to bring about an end of this intolerable colonial regime, even if to do so they would have to sacrifice the dubious military advantages which they derive from their asso-ciation with Portugal?

Earlier a Western observer, Basil Davidson, wrote:

There can be no real doubt that Portugal has used, and is using, NATO armaments in Angola. Without such

NATO supplies, the Portuguese could never have deployed the aircraft, weapons and destructive techniques they have operated and still operate against African men, women and children. Only Norway among the NATO powers has refused to sell arms to Portugal: because, as Foreign Minister Lange said on 21 June, 'Norway regards it as a burden for the whole Western alliance that one member-country seeks to retain colonies by force.'*

Let us see how the involvement of NATO in the Portuguese wars in Africa is justified. In 1963, the commander in chief of the NATO forces, General Lemnitzer, stated: 'The Portuguese soldiers are defending a territory, raw materials and bases which are indispensable not only to the defence of Europe, but also to the whole of the Western world.'

There has been an abundance of official declarations on the strategic value of the Portuguese possessions in Africa, as well as of Portugal herself. For example:

'Both Portugal's situation and the assurance of a stable political regime make this Atlantic coast a base of great importance to the United States.'*

The strategic position of the Azores hardly needs emphasis. The Cape Verde Islands, which hold the key to the southern part of the Atlantic, are no less important as bases, lying as they do off the French West African coast, and on the air route to the South Americas. The large airport on Sal Island is already the nucleus of what may become a strategic wartime base.

Angola and Guinea, with 1,816 kilometres of coastline on the Atlantic, may be regarded as an integral part of Atlantic defence. They also offer a vital outlet to the inland territories of Africa.*

Over a decade later, opinions of the strategic value of

Portugal's possessions were very much the same:

> Portuguese Guinea is the last territory in West Africa
> possessed by a NATO power, and should be considered
> of vital importance for the Cape route and for the West's
> strategy of resistance to tricontinental subversion.*

This is why Portugal was invited into NATO in 1949,
and why today, within the military privacy of NATO,
light and heavy arms, ammunition, napalm, aircraft and
detachments of marines are regularly delivered to Portugal.

In 1949, however, when invited by the United States to
join NATO the Salazar government did so with some
reservations, and indicated clearly that adopting the treaty
did not commit them to adopting its ideological content:

> The definition of this ideology is unfortunate, and
> suffers from vagueness and imprecision in the use of
> certain expressions which have become discredited be-
> cause of the widely differing senses in which they are
> used. We consider ourselves bound by the obligations of
> the Pact and by its general objectives, but not by its
> doctrinaire considerations governing systems whose
> virtues are well known in our country.

In addition there were a number of conditions. Portugal
would keep all her forces for the defence of the Iberian
Peninsula; this new commitment would not detract from
the Treaty of Alliance with Spain; finally, Portugal would
not make any contribution to the troops needed for the
defence of Europe and would not place its airports at their
disposal. In spite of these important reservations, Portugal
was admitted as a member of the Atlantic Alliance in 1949.

The relationship between NATO and Portugal has had
its ups and downs, but overall the marriage has been a
happy one. In 1952 the commander in chief of NATO
forces, General Ridgeway, had to ask Portugal to go beyond
the original agreement and contribute to the troops. In
return the Salazar government increased its demands that

the Portuguese possessions in Africa should be officially considered as part of the NATO sphere of influence. Up to now neither the Salazar regime nor the Caetano government have succeeded. The southern frontier of the NATO zone was originally fixed along the Tropic of Cancer. Thus the Azores come into it but not the Cape Verde Islands, nor the other Portuguese possessions in Africa. Since the question is one of supreme importance to her Portugal has often attempted to have this decision reversed, trying initially to get the Cape Verde Islands at least admitted into the zone. During his last visit to Lisbon, Chancellor Kiesinger voiced his agreement with the idea that Western defence should be extended outside the frontiers of Europe.

When the Portuguese government began to gauge the extent of its difficulties in Africa and to fear that it might simply lose its possessions altogether, it adopted a more conciliatory tone towards its allies. Two Portuguese divisions were placed at their disposal, though on the condition that West Germany should be admitted to NATO and that cooperation agreements should be signed with Franco's Spain. In 1956 these two demands were accepted. General Betelho Moniz, supreme commander of the Portuguese armed forces, announced that a third Portuguese division was to be formed for the defence of Europe. In return, NATO began to supply the Portuguese army with substantial quantities of modern armaments, manufactured in the United States. Also in 1956, the Portuguese government had to place two airports, Espinho and Montijo, at the disposal of the NATO forces.

In 1961, when its fears for the stability of its Overseas Territories turned out to be well founded, relations between the Salazar government and its Atlantic allies became somewhat chilled, particularly with the Kennedy administration in the United States. On several occasions the Americans protested at the use of NATO arms in Angola and of NATO planes for transporting troops. Two Portuguese divisions left the NATO forces for Africa. Recalling

NATO's Hidden Wars 179

the precedent of France's actions in Algeria, the Portuguese Foreign Minister, Franco Nogueira, defended Portugal's right to send troops armed by NATO to Angola.* At the time, the Kennedy administration did not share this point of view. A few months later a NATO commission headed by Admiral Evans was sent to Portugal with the firm intention of investigating the use of NATO forces and armaments in the struggle developing in Angola.

A minor diplomatic war then began; Portugal was soon threatening to leave NATO. In March 1961 the Salazar government recalled all the advantages which Portugal had to offer the Atlantic Club:

- The European zone most closely linked to the United States.
- The free use of the Azores as a base.
- The supply bases of Madeira and the Cape Verde Islands.
- A key position in the Mediterranean with the naval base at Lages and the air bases of Espinho-Esmoritz and Montijo.
- The facilities, in case of war, of an electronic and meteorological communications network without which maritime traffic and anti-submarine measures would be impossible.
- Large reserves of uranium, tungsten and other strategic minerals, as well as the ore reserves available in black Africa.
- The defence of the mouth of the Congo.

It was understood that all these advantages would be lost if Portugal left NATO, or in other words if NATO ceased to give her the aid she wanted. This ultimatum produced a quick reaction. The new Secretary-General of NATO, Dirk Stikker, came to Portugal to reassure Salazar of the support of his European allies. 'We must combine our strength against the communist threat,' he said.

Shortly afterwards, Governor-General Silva Tavares declared his satisfaction at the part NATO was playing in the African wars. 'The men of NATO are carrying out acts of real heroism in the fight against the barbarian hordes,' he said on 14 June 1961, on passing over his command to his successor Silva Freire.

The crisis was over; Portugal was still in NATO. On several occasions since then, the Portuguese government, under Salazar and under Caetano, has pleaded the importance of its African wars, either to be exempted from some of the duties incumbent on Portugal as a member of NATO, or to obtain increased aid. The successive ministers of defence have almost invariably pronounced themselves satisfied with the comprehension shown at their predicament, and every negotiation has always been brought to a positive conclusion. Thus the Portuguese government did not miss the chance of bargaining when the Azores Treaty came up for renewal in 1962. Apart from 'financial aid': 'The United States have offered several warships, as well as other equipment which Portugal badly needs for the defence of her Overseas Territories. And all this in exchange for a renewal of the lease on the Azores base.'*

One wonders if the 'financial aid' was the 80 million dollars a year quoted in American newspapers at the time. At any rate there was a sum of 50 million dollars agreed in 1962 by the American Import-Export Bank. Also an agreement covering the building of warships had to be extended to cover the price of three of them. Finally, in January 1963, the United States announced the delivery of thirty aircraft, followed in May by a consignment of aircraft engines for the Portuguese Air Force.

The Portuguese government seemed well satisfied. On 4 January 1963, the Azores Treaty was temporarily renewed, but with the Portuguese government still retaining the right to rescind it at six months' notice. As a result, the American administration is under constant pressure from Portugal. American aid has been increased in the past few years, in the form of payments 'for the military base', despite the protests of the Senate, which has considered this aid excessive. Negotiations over the Azores were to be concluded by the end of 1971.

What in fact is Portugal's role in NATO? The geographic area covered by the North Atlantic Treaty is divided among the Canada-United States Regional Planning Group – which is responsible for North American defence – and three Commands: the European Command, the Channel Command, and the Atlantic Ocean Command, headed by the Supreme Allied Commander, Atlantic, or SACLANT. Portugal comes under this third command and another subordinate command, IBERLANT, which is centred in Lisbon itself.

SACLANT

The headquarters of SACLANT are at Norfolk, Virginia, in the United States. Its general staff consists of 150 officers belonging to the armies, navies, air forces and marines of the NATO countries. It is at Norfolk that studies are carried out on the naval support of the European Command, in particular the protection of the strategically important Atlantic islands such as Iceland, Greenland, the Azores, Madeira, the Bermudas and the Faroes. SACLANT controls a zone 'stretching from the Arctic to the Tropic of Cancer and territorial waters which extend from North America to the coasts of Europe and Africa, and thus of Portugal'.

The tasks of SACLANT in time of war are firstly to 'guarantee the security of the whole of the Atlantic Ocean, protecting the maritime routes and preventing the enemy from penetrating them', and secondly to take care of 'the defence of the islands situated in the Atlantic Ocean'. Among these islands, Iceland and the Azores are covered by special provisions. Having no army, Iceland, in time of war, is placed directly under NATO command.

The same goes for the Azores, and such a provision is completely without precedent. There is nothing like it covering any of the other territories of the countries of the Atlantic Alliance. The archipelago is a strategic point of prime importance, at least for a policy of 'Atlantic domination' as understood by the United States. It already houses the naval air base at Lagos, the NATO installations on the island of São Miguel, the French missile control base on the island of Flores and a testing station for experiments in submarine acoustics financed by the eight NATO countries. It is hardly surprising that the Azores should be directly controlled by NATO, in time of war at the very least.

According to a statement made by Colonel Sousa Meneses at a session of the Portuguese National Assembly in December 1969, their total value amounts to £14½ million sterling, of which £1½ million represents the Portuguese contribution. The oldest and still the most important installation in the Azores is the Lagos air base. Between 1951 and 1957, this base cost 100 million dollars, to which must be added the loans made to the Portuguese government in exchange for renewing the lease.

But the installations in the Azores are not the only NATO bases on Portuguese territory. In Portugal itself there is also a satellite tracking station belonging to the American navy, the Polaris submarine base at Vila Praia da Vitoria, the West German air base at Beja, the English air base on the Tagus, and, finally, the most recent installation, the headquarters of IBERLANT, the Iberian Atlantic Regional Command near Lisbon.

Although all the NATO bases were negotiated with the Salazar government on terms favourable to Portugal, their presence nevertheless gives rise to protests from a whole sector of Portuguese opinion, including a number of staunch supporters of the regime. Perhaps the big Portuguese families are afraid that this impressive show of force will be turned against them if one day the members of NATO decide they can no longer bear the cost of Portugal's policies in Africa, or her antidemocratic excesses at home.

Although they are in effect supporting these policies, some of the countries have at times shown their disapproval of them. Finally, the NATO presence is obviously a threat to the government in Lisbon. However, this is a price which the latter is obviously prepared to pay, since it seems unable to do without the material aid offered in compensation.

IBERLANT

The Iberian Atlantic Command, or IBERLANT, had been planned long before it was actually set up. For a long time this particular geographic area remained 'uncovered' in NATO military strategy since the allies were not too sure where to establish the headquarters of the command. Gibraltar and Brest had both been considered. Then France left NATO and a new strategic situation was created in Europe. Finally, in February 1967, the decision was made to set up IBERLANT at Lisbon. It still has no permanent headquarters, but is currently established at Rio Mouro, a few kilometres from the capital. 'France's withdrawal and the absence of Spain from NATO meant that Portugal was at an enormous geographical distance from the other European member-countries,'* stated the *Diario de Lisboa*, and the NATO news bulletin added: 'The Command ... has been set up in Portugal to fill the strategic vacuum created in southern Europe by France's withdrawal from NATO integrated forces.'*

The result of France's withdrawal was to bring about a closer collaboration between the other Mediterranean countries – such as Greece and Italy – and NATO, and to lend renewed importance to the American bases in Spain. The setting up of IBERLANT in Lisbon formed part of this framework and gave Portugal a fundamental role in American strategy.

The zone controlled by IBERLANT is that enclosed by the 42nd parallel in the north, the 20° meridian in the west, the Tropic of Cancer in the south and the African coast, the Straits of Gibraltar, the south coast of Spain and the Spanish-Portuguese border in the east. In this zone the naval and military commands at Gibraltar and Madeira are subordinate to the central command at Lisbon.

The general functions of IBERLANT were reported in somewhat vague terms by the *Diario de Lisboa* in the year of its creation:

> The IBERLANT zone will play a role of prime importance in time of war and have a permanent task of organisation and preparation of the services in time of peace.... [In time of war] all sea and air traffic will be forbidden, and the necessary precautions will be taken to prevent the enemy from gaining access to the peninsula. It will thus be possible to obtain greater cooperation between the NATO Armed Forces and to effect local 'control' and better protection of navigation. It will also be possible to create points of defence against acts of aggression from the Atlantic and also from the Mediterranean, where the naval perspective has recently undergone a number of undeniably important alterations.*

One thing at least emerges clearly – IBERLANT has the task of meeting any 'acts of aggression' against the Iberian peninsula, coming from the Atlantic or the Mediterranean. What it in fact does is to control access to the Mediterranean – a fact amply demonstrated by the various naval and air manoeuvres carried out in the access area by Portugal, the United States and Spain, and the manoeuvres carried out off Madeira at the end of March 1969, involving twenty-five warships belonging to the NATO countries.

The United States' interest in this area is so obvious that Portugal has even considered negotiating the use of another valuable strategic point, the island of Madeira. On 25 April 1969 the Portuguese defence minister, General Sa Vania Rebelo, made the following statement:

> In this year, which is the twentieth anniversary of the

Atlantic Alliance, it may be appropriate to point out the considerable value of this island in relation to this alliance, and the importance of the combined positions of Lisbon and Funchal (capital of Madeira) in defending access to the Mediterranean, especially when we consider the presence of the Russian squadron in our seas. Consequently a NATO Command under IBERLANT, which controls this south-western sector of the North Atlantic, has been established here in Lisbon. But in view of the area's importance, it is also necessary to have military installations in Madeira corresponding to its strategic mission.

One wonders whether this statement gave rise to new negotiations between Portugal and the United States, with a view to giving the Americans access to the island of Madeira. Certainly more 'Atlantic' personalities have visited the Portuguese government in the past two years than ever before. The American admirals Baynes, Gralla, Homes and Rivero, and numerous British, Dutch and Italian officers belonging to the general staffs of the NATO commands have visited Portugal and NATO's military installations there. Dozens of American and allied warships visit the Portuguese ports, and these visits are almost always the occasion for air-sea manoeuvres involving the Portuguese army.

Everything seems to point to an increase in Portuguese participation in NATO's strategic plans in the near future. And this, of course, means increased aid for Portuguese colonial policies – whether direct or indirect – in order to ensure the survival of the regime.

Many of the official US statements denying American support of Portugal's colonial wars were exposed by the US Administration itself when on 11 August 1973 (see *The Observer* of 12 August 1973) the Pentagon disclosed that for the past three years Portuguese Air Force officers, mostly fighter pilots, had been trained at US bases in

Germany and that 'some of them have been sent to fight in Portugal's colonial wars'.

Seventy-nine such Portuguese flyers had been trained in Germany and twenty-five others in the USA – 'to learn US techniques in flying combat support missions'.

The Cost of Helping Portugal

It is difficult to estimate exactly how much direct and indirect aid the various NATO countries have given Portugal. But it is known that the chief donors are the United States, France, West Germany and Britain.

The United States

Let us first of all consider the various treaties which have been signed between the United States and Portugal. First of all there is a mutual defence treaty drawn up in 1951, completed in September of the same year, then extended to the use of the Azores in November 1957 and renewed in 1962. In addition a treaty concerning the replacement of defence equipment was signed in July 1952 and amended in September 1960, and an agreement concerning a programme of arms production was also drawn up in September 1960. Some of these agreements were signed in 1960 when it had already become clear that Portugal did not intend to grant her African possessions their independence, and was ready to go to war over them. Towards the end of 1960 the United States agreed to finance the construction of two substantial warships for the Portuguese government. 'Portugal now has a duty to defend her Overseas Territories,' declared the naval minister Admiral Quintanilha e Mendonça Dias, 'and the American aid will facilitate our task and help to iron out some of our difficulties.' According to the Mutual Defence Assistance Agreement, dated 5 January 1951, the aim of such measures would be to 'reinforce international peace and security within the framework of the United Nations Charter', while recognising 'the increased confidence of the free peoples of the world in their capacity for resisting aggression'. In this same treaty, conditions were laid down expressly controlling the terms of any military aid:

Each government must make effective use of the aid received in furthering the defence of the North Atlantic zone, to facilitate the application of the aims of the North Atlantic Treaty, in accordance with the defence plans formulated by NATO and agreed by the two governments.

Thus, by the terms of this agreement, the American aid should never have been diverted from its original aim; Portugal should never have been able to make use of arms given her within the context of NATO to fight her African wars.

The quantity of armaments supplied to Portugal under this treaty was considerable. During the period 1949 to 1951 Portugal received a total of 370 million dollars from the United States, out of which 80 million were in the form of economic aid and 290 million in the form of military aid. It was clearly specified at the time that if these arms were used in the colonies, the agreements would be broken off. However, in the years which followed, the United States frequently had occasion to note that Portugal was not adhering faithfully to the agreements. Numerous reports by journalists and commissions of experts warned the United States or NATO that these arms were being used in the colonies – without this leading to any serious reprisals against the Lisbon government. Indeed, in August 1961 a resolution had to be passed by Congress whereby the United States would continue its military aid to Portugal. (It is perhaps significant that this mutual assistance treaty between the two countries includes an agreement on the part of the Portuguese government to 'facilitate the production and transfer to the United States of all the raw materials or semi-finished items produced by Portugal or the territories under its administration, which the United States may need'.)

At that time relations between the United States and Portugal were at a high point: in May 1960, Eisenhower passed through Lisbon and paid undisguised homage to the Salazar regime. A few months later, when the United Nations proposed to conduct an inquiry on the situation in the Portuguese colonies, the Eisenhower administration abstained from voting.

But things changed with the accession of Kennedy. On 15 March 1961 the United States supported a vote in the UN Security Council demanding an inquiry in Angola. On 20 April the UN General Assembly called for sweeping reforms in Angola in order to bring the country towards independence. The Portuguese reaction was not slow in coming. 'Spontaneous' anti-American demonstrations took place in the streets of Luanda on 22 March and in Lisbon on 28 March.

The United States did not climb down, however, and together with the Soviet Union demanded that Portugal should put an end to the reign of terror in Angola. American aid dropped from 25 million dollars to 3 million dollars. All arms sales to Portugal were suspended. In November 1961 the United States denied, in the UN General Assembly, that American arms supplied to Portugal by NATO were being used in Angola – only to admit it a year later in the same place. Portugal remained unembarrassed.

The Lisbon government let the storm pass over and then counter-attacked. If the United States persisted in their denigrating attitude towards the Portuguese colonial wars, it was hinted, then they must expect to lose their Free Europe radio station, based in Lisbon, which broadcast to the eastern countries, and they might also lose the Azores base. We have already seen how much the Portuguese regime obtained from the Americans for this base, and by what methods.

In the face of this ultimatum from Lisbon the United States finally capitulated, and their policy underwent a complete *volte-face*. In 1962 a loan of 50 million dollars was allocated by the American Import-Export Bank. The agreements covering the construction of a warship, of which the Americans were going to pay half, were extended to cover three ships instead of one, which represented an additional gift of 5 million dollars. In January 1963 it was announced that Portugal would take delivery of thirty Cessna T-37C aircraft, eighteen of which wholly paid for by MAP – the Military Assistance Programme of the United States. In theory these aircraft were to be used for pilot training and internal security; in fact the type is currently used in Vietnam because of its short take-off capability, and the aircraft in question were delivered completely equipped for anti-guerilla warfare.

The Azores crisis was almost over and, with the signing of the new treaty in January 1963, American aid began to increase once more, this time disguised as aid 'within the framework of NATO military agreements'. Moreover, when the US Congress decided to end all military aid to Western Europe in October 1963, an exception was made for Portugal – and Spain. Voices were raised in Congress and in the Senate, pointing out that Portugal had already received too much in return for the Azores base. In fact, for the period 1962 to 1968, the official figures mention some 33·7 million dollars' worth of military aid to Portugal, to which should be added various unspecified sums allocated under the heading of 'defence support'.

During the year 1962 American policy towards Portugal changed. In January of that year the United States were upholding the Angolans' right to independence in the UN, and demanding that Portugal should end the reign of terror in that area. In December the same government voted against a resolution condemning the Portuguese policy in Africa, and asking all the powers to stop selling arms to the Lisbon government. This latter position is still in force. The

Kennedy administration had taken sides with the NATO members who had always been strong supporters of Portugal.

By January 1962 outside observers could watch Portuguese planes bomb and strafe African villages, visit the charred remains of towns like Mbanza M'Pangu and M'Pangala and copy the data from 750-pound napalm bomb casings from which the Portuguese had not removed the labels marked 'Property US Air Force'.*

Today, when the US government is asked whether it is aware that American arms are being used in Africa, it replies that its consulate in Luanda is quite unable to check the fact.

The United States not only sends arms but also technical assistance on quite a large scale. Since 1951 the Military Assistance Advisory Group (MAAG), consisting of twenty American military personnel and five civilians, has been stationed in Portugal, where it has the task of replacing faulty equipment, training Portuguese military personnel and faithfully reporting the results obtained.

At a press conference at the beginning of 1963 the US Secretary of State for Africa, Mennen Williams, tried to convince journalists that the United States had never proclaimed their support of liberation in Angola, and stated that he himself was convinced that Portugal was making every effort to improve the situation there. Six months later, in Chicago, Mennen Williams admitted: 'It is not in our interests for Portugal to leave Africa or diminish its influence in that area.' It was at this time that the CIA was supporting the movement of Robert Holden.

In the meantime, cooperation between the countries continued to increase. When the Caetano government came into power in 1968, negotiations over the Azores base were reopened at its request. The military base had meanwhile been extended and as compensation Portugal demanded 200 million dollars' worth of arms, to be delivered over a period of five years.

Napalm and phosphorus bombs marked 'Made in USA' have been dropped on African villages not far from here, according to numerous eyewitness reports and photographs which appear to be genuine.

The villages are part of the Guinean territory wrested from Portuguese control by nationalist forces.*

Addressing a conference organised in Lusaka on 18 January 1972 by the African-American Institute and the School of Advanced International Studies of Johns Hopkins University to make Americans more aware of Africa, President Kaunda stated that US treaty obligations with Portugal stood in the way of active American participation in the removal of colonialism from Africa. 'No major power genuinely committed to peace and the welfare of mankind can ignore the unfolding crisis in this part of the world,' he added.

According to figures released at the end of 1971 by the Stockholm International Peace Research Institute (SIPRI), known US aid to Portugal included F-84G and F-86F fighters, and probably as many as 150 T-6G Texans, and T.Mk.3 Harvard Trainers, some of which were supplied through the UK; 40 Lockheed PV-2 Harpoons and several transports, including a large number of C-47s and numerous other types; and 30 armed T-37C (already mentioned above). The F-84G fighter squadron is based in Luanda, where are also to be found most of PV-2 Harpoons used for bombing operations. There are also mine-sweepers, patrol boats and a frigate built under US offshore procurement in France, Portugal and Italy, and two frigates whose lease was renewed in 1962. The USA further delivered, in 1966 and 1967, three more frigates (already mentioned above) as well as M-41, M-47 and M4 tanks, and M-16 half-track armoured personnel carriers and probably 155mm howitzers.

This, of course, is what is known as 'official' aid; that more aid goes undercover was illustrated when Portugal requested 29 B-26 bombers to form a light bombing unit for operations in Angola and Mozambique. Although the request was turned down by the US State Department, 7 B-26s with spare parts arrived in Portugal a year later. A pilot, who was tried for smuggling these planes out of the US without proper licences, claimed that deliveries had taken place with the knowledge of the CIA. The pilot, incidentally, was acquitted.

To this must be added the significant delivery, decided on in September 1970, of two Boeing 707 jets to the Portuguese by the USA, without specifications as to the areas where this type of plane (used for the transport of troops and equipment) could operate. Previously, the State Department would specify in the case of such deliveries that these could be used for 'civilian' purposes only by the Portuguese airlines TAP. On 12 October 1971 the *Tribuna*, of Mozambique, announced that 'the Portuguese air force is about to take delivery of two Boeing 707s ... with registration numbers 6801 and 6802'. The Portuguese paper went on to say that these American planes would be 'used to transport troops between Lisbon and the African Provinces'. These planes are already being used by the TAP and the DETA (Mozambique) airlines which have both signed service contracts with the Portuguese High Command. Following the acquisition of these aeroplanes, Lisbon decided to cut troop transport by sea drastically; in 1970, an explosion had taken place on board the *Cunene* with troops bound for Mozambique, and in the same year still another explosion took place in the docks of Lisbon where the *Niassa* was embarking troops and material for Mozambique. Then, in 1971, the world was startled with the mysterious disappearance off Mozambique of the *Angoche*, which carried fuel for helicopters and other material. The purchase of the two Boeing 707s, costing a total of 18.5 million dollars, together 'with additional material' was made possible through a loan of 4,172,850 dollars from the Export-Import Bank to the TAP, in January 1970. Earlier, a 15·2 million dollar loan from America had allowed Portugal to purchase three Super-Constellations and one Boeing 727.

France

The Portuguese army has developed a modern system for dealing with guerillas which the Americans, the French and the English consider perfect and which has brought about a total change in military strategy. We have taken our lessons not only from the French experiences in Indo-China and North Africa, but also from the methods used by the German army in combating the resistance movements in France and Russia.*

To make sure that the lessons of Indo-China and Algeria are well learned, Portuguese officers and their subordinates are trained for the anti-guerilla struggle by the French army in France. France is in fact the biggest supplier of arms to Portugal after the USA, but unlike the other countries, the French government does not impose any restrictions on their use. Moreover, this open support of Portuguese colonial policies has never been discussed in the Assemblée Nationale. Paris makes no bones about the fact that sale of arms serves her 'commercial interests'. But there was still another reason for this military cooperation between Paris and Lisbon.

What is Portugal able to offer the French in exchange for these arms? In 1963, General de Gaulle launched the project of a national *force de frappe*. At this point the French needed a tracking station for their missile installation in south-western France. After negotiations with Portugal they were able to build one in the Azores, which was opened in 1965. In addition to the installations at the base itself, 152 kilometres of road was built. The project also involved enlarging the port of Santa Cruz and building a hydro-electric power station. About a hundred Frenchmen are said to be employed at the base.

In exchange for these facilities, France supplies Portugal with practically all the arms and the military equipment, especially that suited for counter-insurgency, which the latter sees fit to ask for; tanks, armoured carriers, helicopters, warships, arms and ammunition are all delivered to Portugal for use in Africa. The Portuguese colonial air force has all of its helicopter units equipped with French helicopters – the Alouette II (about thirty, mounted with rockets), the Alouette III, equipped with AS.11 and AS.12 air-to-surface missiles (about eighty are believed to have been already delivered) and the terrible SA-330 Puma, which is a joint Anglo-French production. This helicopter is already being used for assault operations in the African colonies. The Portuguese government is extremely happy with the French helicopters and has never made any mystery of their use in Africa, and this has in any case been confirmed by numerous photographs and reports.

Nord-Aviation has supplied a certain number of military transport and fighter aircraft. These aircraft were either delivered directly, like the six 2502 Noratlases supplied in 1962, or through the intermediary of the Union Aéronautique Transatlantique (UAT). Four Holste Broussard transport planes and a few Junkers Ju 52s were also delivered in 1960-61.

The French naval dockyards have also benefited from Portuguese orders. In 1954-5 the United States ordered three patrol vessels from them on Portugal's behalf. In 1964 a major deal for eight units – four frigates and four submarines of the 'Daphne' class – was concluded for the value of $100 million with a long-term financial guarantee from the French government. The frigates, built to accommodate helicopters and marines, were used for COIN (counter-insurgency) operations in Guinea Bissao. Army equipment of French origin, such as the AML 60 armoured cars, mortars, machine-guns, hand grenades, etc., is also being used by Portugal in her colonial wars.

The French firm of Barbier, Bernard et Turenne S.A.

supply substantial quantities of electronic equipment and practically all the lighting for Portuguese airports in the 'Overseas Territories'.

All these supplies are paid for on long-term credit. The French government grants payment facilities ranging from ten to twenty years – at 6 per cent annual interest however – and acts as Portugal's financial guarantor *vis-à-vis* the French firms.

France, who it should be mentioned *en passant* was now involved in manufacturing the 'Crotale' guided missile system for South Africa – where the system is known as 'Cactus' – is in fact the western country cooperating the most closely in the military field with Lisbon and Pretoria. Nevertheless, on 28 April 1973, the Foreign Minister M. Jobert unabashedly reiterated the official line that France 'sells no arms' for Portugal's African wars.

Earlier, on 23 April, in a press statement in Paris, OAU's Assistant Secretary-General Mohammed Sahnoun had branded France as the 'racists' best ally'.

Significantly, it was announced in Paris again, end of September 1973, that France would now sell Mirages ... to Zaïre also giving the necessary technical assistance and training pilots as well. 17 Mirages were to be sold to General Mobutu, as 'a first sale'.

West Germany

Although Portugal has not made any substantial contribution to the tasks of NATO because of our struggle in the Overseas Territories, our allies have always shown great understanding over our position.*

Among the NATO allies the German Federal Republic has always shown, and still shows, a truly remarkable 'understanding' towards Portugal. And she has good reasons for doing so.

In 1952, it was the Portuguese Defence minister, Santos Costa, who pleaded the cause of West Germany with

NATO, and demanded her unconditional admittance to the organisation. In the years which followed, it was a Portuguese minister – first Santos Costa, then his successor, Da Cunha – who repeated the demand each time. And when, in 1955, Germany was finally admitted to NATO, the Lisbon government welcomed the news 'so warmly that there was general surprise abroad'.

There are a number of treaties governing relations between Portugal and the German Federal Republic. In 1959 it was decided that Portugal would supply West Germany with military facilities in exchange for German rockets and precision instruments. In 1960 Germany was granted permission to establish an important air base at Beja. In 1961 a Committee for German-Portuguese Cooperation was set up. A military treaty was ratified in 1963, under cover of which Portugal was subsequently to receive all her supplies of arms and military equipment from West Germany. In 1965 the two countries signed an extradition treaty, and in 1966 a 'cultural treaty'. In the latter it was stated, for example, that 'school books both in West Germany and in Portugal should not contain texts which may give a bad impression of the history, the cultural values or life in the other country'.

It is obviously the military treaty of June 1962 which deserves the closest attention. Although the text of this treaty has never been made public it is known to have allowed for a base and stocking facilities for the Luftwaffe at Beja. And a training centre for the Bundeswehr at Sta. Margarida, where a German division at reduced strength – the 'Zentrale Deutsche Verbindungsstelle in Portugal' (ZDVP) – is permanently stationed. It consists of about 100 men commanded by a general. In exchange, Portugal received substantial military assistance in every field. The Beja base, about 150 kms. south of Lisbon, is a vast airfield covering some 800 hectares, equipped with two runways, each three kilometres long, hangars, stores, a hospital, barracks and accommodation for 500 families. This complex, costing $40 million, of which over $37 million was paid by Bonn and less than $3 million by Lisbon, is West Germany's only military base abroad. F-104G Starfighters, Fiat G-91s, C-160 Transaals, 2051D Noratlas transports, as well as other types of aeroplanes, can be fully maintained and repaired at Beja. All these aeroplanes are used in the colonies. A huge depot was built at Castelloas with a port nearby, which was conveniently described as a 'tourist port'. A powerful centre of communications was set up at Evora which allows direct communication between the German base in Portugal and the Bundeswehr high command in Bonn. Portuguese technicians are used in Beja by the Germans to install and repair electronic equipment. West German bombers having taken part in the strafing of a village named Djagali in Guinea Bissao, the West Berlin trade union paper *Tribune** wrote on 1 July 1966: 'The manoeuvre ground for training the Federal German Luftwaffe under wartime conditions is obviously to be Portuguese Guinea, Angola and Mozambique'. The reader will better understand the usefulness of Portugal and her colonies to the Luftwaffe since it lacks airspace in West Germany for training purposes.

The total value of arms so far delivered to Portugal by West Germany is estimated at $100 million and there is further German military assistance of some $3 million per year.

When, beginning in 1966, West Germany sold 40 Fiat G-91Rs from surplus Luftwaffe stocks, the German Ministry of Defence explained that this sale had taken place 'on the basis of the principle of mutual aid between NATO partners' and that the delivery had been subject to a clause whereby these aeroplanes would be 'used exclusively in Portugal for defence purposes within the framework of the North Atlantic Pact'.

A spokesman for the Portuguese Foreign Ministry was to reply however: 'The transaction was agreed within the spirit of the North Atlantic Pact. It was agreed that the

planes would be used only for defensive purposes within
Portuguese territory. Portuguese territory extends to Africa
– Angola, Mozambique and Portuguese Guinea.'* Bonn –
and for that matter the rest of NATO members – remain
silent.

The Fiat G-91 fighter aircraft – originally built for
NATO with an Italian airframe, an English engine, a
French undercarriage and German electronic equipment –
was obtained by Portugal after Canada's refusal to let West
Germany sell to Portugal Sabre fighters of Canadian origin,
because Lisbon would not satisfactorily guarantee to the
Canadian government that these planes would not be used
in Africa. Portugal obtained from West Germany some 65
G-91s and these planes, which were quickly transferred to
the colonies, first formed the Esquadra 52 stationed in
Guinea and later transferred to Beira.

Germany also delivered to Portugal 110 Dornier Do-27s
used in Africa for both liaison and ground operations.*
Some of these planes supplied in 1969 went to Portugal via
Belgium after use in Katanga. Fouga Magisters and Sabres
have also been used by the Portuguese Air Force in the
colonies, although the German government denies having
sold these to Portugal. The key to this mystery was discovered by two Brazilian journalists who announced that
the Brazilian government had negotiated the purchase of
Fouga Magisters from Germany with the intention of re-
selling them to Portugal.* A German helicopter, the Saro
Skeeter, is also used by the Portuguese. Twelve Nord 2051D
Noratlas' are used as parachute transports, and twenty
Transaal C-160s are known to have been sold to Portugal
for use in the colonies.

Army material has also been supplied, in particular
heavy Mercedes Benz trucks and the G-3 rifle, of which 160
a day were being manufactured under German licence at
the Braco da Prata factory. A fair number of these rifles
have been captured by Liberation Movements in the
colonies.

Nor has the Portuguese navy been neglected by the Bonn government. Six warships of 1,400 tons, the largest to be built in Germany since the war, have been constructed, or are under construction, for Portugal in the naval dockyard at Hamburg; they will cost 40 million dollars. According to the *Revista de Marinha* of May 1960: 'These ships are provided with helicopters, and will be equipped for prolonged service at sea in order to support our fleet of patrol boats.'

Starting in 1968, Germany's interest in the Beja base ran into problems. Spain was protesting against the use of her airspace by German military aeroplanes operating from Portugal and German public opinion was beginning to protest against the use of these aircraft in colonial wars. Then difficulties began with Portuguese personnel, whom the stricter Luftwaffe men were finding badly trained and incompetent. Relations between Bonn and Lisbon were being clouded. With a hint of naïvety, a German newspaper expressed general discontent in these terms:

> The German Luftwaffe will probably never be able to use the military base at Beja, and this project, which has cost hundreds of millions appears to be a senseless scandal. What is more, the financial needs of our Portuguese allies seem to be never-ending. All they want is money, money and more money, and this attitude on the part of a 'hospitable' country is particularly outrageous.*

In the light of a new agreement in 1968 on Beja, it was decided that aircrews for the German civil airline, Lufthansa, would be trained at Beja. However, the real content of this agreement has never been published, but it appeared that operational activity of the Luftwaffe might be resumed at Beja, where the secondment of part of a transport squadron was planned in 1971. Moreover, Germany would continue to run the Alveria aeronautical establishment.

But 1968 was only a temporary crisis, a passing cloud in the sky of the generally very cordial relations between the two countries. In 1968 the Federal German Defence Committee recommended that deliveries of military supplies already ordered should be carried out. At the same time it was stated that any new offer of armaments on Portugal's part could not be accepted until 1973, as Germany was already well supplied. In addition, the delivery of 200 new military aircraft to Portugal was accompanied by discreet provisos as to their subsequent use. In 1970 the first of three patrol boats ordered by Portugal was delivered.

To this substantial military aid must be added the various loans Germany has made to the Portuguese government; to mention just a few, there was one of 40 million dollars in 1961, of 35 million dollars in 1962 and 15 million dollars in 1963.

Great Britain

When the British government considered using the Azores as a base during the Second World War an old treaty was dug up dating from 1373 which concerned military alliance between Portugal and England. The principle of this treaty was confirmed at the beginning of the war, and reaffirmed on 12 October 1943, as a result of which Portugal was congratulated on numerous occasions on the assistance she had given the Allied forces. In 1945 the Salazar government received 3 million dollars' worth of military equipment from the British government. A few months later Major Luzi de Camera Pine announced, in the Portuguese National Assembly, that under the new Azores treaty Portugal would receive 45 million dollars' worth of aid from Great Britain.

Cooperation between the two countries chiefly concerns the navy. Before the war the British navy had founded modern naval schools in Portugal and supplied a certain number of boats. After the war Great Britain continued to be Portugal's largest supplier of warships; and numerous Portuguese officers go through the Royal Naval colleges.

Nevertheless, after the outbreak of the struggle in

Angola, the British government decided under pressure from Parliament to put a stop to arms exports to Portugal and her colonies. They did not, however, stop deliveries made under the cover of NATO. In this way two warships were delivered, the *D. Francisco Almeida* and the *Vasco da Gama*. 'These ships will help Portugal to fulfil her obligations towards NATO,' said Harold Macmillan in parliament, adding: 'I doubt if they will make much difference to the sad situation in Angola.' However, in December 1961, the Portuguese *Revista de Marinha* welcomed the delivery of the two ships and announced that they would soon be used in the Overseas Territories. The *D. Francisco de Almeida* was in Mozambique during the same period. The next ship, the patrol boat *Regulus*, a British hull fitted in Portugal, was sent directly to Angola. In total, Britain delivered four frigates, and a number of minesweepers, patrol boats and submarines.

Also, despite its declarations, the British government sent more than 150 disassembled Auster D.5/160 utility light aircraft to Portugal between 1961 and 1964. Almost all of these aircraft were used in the colonies. In 1963 Portugal ordered replacement parts for them and the cost was entered under 'overseas expenses'. In 1965 Great Britain delivered 200 Austin jeeps to the Portuguese army, still 'within the framework of the NATO' agreements. Armed T.6 Harvard trainers for COIN operations in Africa were also sent by Britain, who has also supplied army equipment, namely armoured cars and the 8·6 inch 'M.20' rocket launcher.

SIX

The Colonies and the Church

The Rome Conference and the audience with the Pope
On 27, 28 and 29 June 1970, an International Conference in Support of the Peoples of the Portuguese Colonies was officially held in Rome, with the full consent of the Italian government.

It was the first time that a member of NATO had shown any concern for the liberation movements in Angola, Guinea and Mozambique, and, to this extent, that the conference took place at all was a defeat for Portuguese policies and those of NATO. The Portuguese government inevitably put pressure on the Italian government, through their ambassador in Rome, to stop the conference from taking place. But several months earlier, at the request of Zambia, the Italian government had already shown that it was favourably disposed towards the cause of the colonised peoples by withdrawing its financial support from the dam project at Cabora Bassa. And once more Italy adopted a more realistic attitude by agreeing to act as host to the Rome Conference, which was important both in terms of the status of the participants (which included a United Nations representative) and of the decisions taken. Ironically enough the conference took place in the same hall where the Council of Ministers of NATO countries had met a few weeks earlier, protected by a spectacular security guard.

The three independence movements in the Portuguese

colonies were represented by their respective leaders – Agostinho Neto, president of the MPLA, Amilcar Cabral, secretary general of the PAIGC, and Marcelina Dos Santos, vice-president of the FRELIMO.

In 1948 Amilcar Cabral had written: 'It is perhaps still too early to write the history of the liberation struggle in the Portuguese colonies; those who one day do so will not be able to forget the wall of silence raised around our peoples by Portuguese colonialism.'

The Conference of Rome broke this silence, and its resolutions were broadcast in all the countries concerned by the Portuguese colonial problem. These resolutions were:

- Condemnation of Portuguese colonialism.
- Condemnation of the aid given to Portugal by NATO, the United States, the German Federal Republic, the United Kingdom and France.
- Condemnation of the alliance of fascists in Pretoria, Salisbury and Lisbon.
- Condemnation of the activities of the groups of financiers who are exploiting the resources and the peoples of Angola, Guinea Bissao, the Cape Verde Islands and Mozambique.
- Recognition of the powers of State sovereignty exercised by the MPLA, the PAIGC and the FRELIMO over vast areas of their countries.
- The need to increase available information about the struggles.
- The duty to organise and develop material support for the liberation struggles and for the work of national reconstruction in Angola, Guinea Bissao and Mozambique.

Religion at gunpoint

On 1 July 1970, a few days after the Rome Conference, Agostinho Neto, Amilcar Cabral and Marcelino Dos Santos were received by Pope Paul VI at the Holy See.

A measure of the significance of this event is to be found in the repercussions it provoked in Portugal. According to a statement made by Marcelo Caetano on 7 July 1970:

> Taking advantage of a routine event in the Pontiff's life, namely the weekly collective audience given to visitors, the terrorists insinuated themselves into the Pope's presence as Catholics and Christians, engaged him in a discussion which could scarcely be heard and later used this for spectacular effect with the aim of compromising our country.

This version of the story deceived no one. It was an obvious manoeuvre designed to minimise the pope's role in the affair, and brought an answer from Radio Vatican stating:

> That the audience of the leaders of the three movements struggling against the Portuguese authorities in Africa was only able to take place by prior consent; that the delegates of the Decolonisation Committee of UNO had attended the anti-colonialist conference in Rome, in company with the leaders of the liberation movements; that the attitude of the Church towards the independence of the new nations remains unchanged and is well known through the documents of the Council, the encyclicals and the allocutions of Paul VI.

Portugal's attempts to sabotage the audience with the pope had already given rise to another incident, when a Portuguese priest insisted in acting as interpreter during the audience itself. Amilcar Cabral indicated to the pope that Neto, Dos Santos and himself were quite capable of conversing with him directly in French, Portuguese or English. The Portuguese priest no longer needed as an interpreter, nevertheless succeeded in preventing any photographs being taken of this historic event.

The Vatican's intervention, though coming rather late in the day, had the merit not only of bringing Portugal's colonial problems to the attention of Christians throughout the world, but also of serving as a warning to the Portuguese clergy. For it is in the name of Christ and the Virgin that the Portuguese government sends its soldiers to fight 'against communism' in the colonies. It would therefore have been rather difficult to explain to these same soldiers why the pope had received the three 'communist' leaders at the Holy See. Indeed, the Portuguese clergy, supported by the established clergy in most of the African countries, even including Zambia, made every effort to falsify the pope's words. For the Catholic Church has not always been so benevolent towards such liberation movements; in fact, in the history of Portuguese colonialism in Africa, it has always taken sides with the occupier, with the rich against the poor, with colonialism against human freedom. From the very start the Catholic missionaries always firmly supported military action against rebellious native populations. We have only to listen to these words from a missionary of the Order of the Holy Ghost:

Without social and political peace, there are not the conditions either for work or for the progress of peoples – progress on the intellectual, moral, educational and religious levels. The mission needs these conditions if it is to prosper – it needs to have the confidence of the peoples it is trying to convert. This is why, at the end of the nineteenth century, when rebellion broke out at Cuanhama, Cubango, Libolo, Dembos, we were in the front line, giving the mission's support to the work of pacification and understanding, to Artur Paiva, Pereira d'Eça, Pais Brandão, João de Almeida and so many other illustrious military leaders. On the territory of Cuanhama, in June 1885, the mission was pillaged and the missionaries massacred. The furniture, the food, even the zinc from the roofs, were all shared out by the attackers. But as we are stubborn we went back there in 1909, and we are still there today, hard at work, our eyes fixed on the future.

Later, in 1933, the Colonial Act drawn up by Dr Salazar and reviving the ideas of João Belo, gave the Church the task of influencing the native populations by means of religion, since 'the simple, untouched minds of these peoples' were 'particularly susceptible to being influenced by religious activity'. At that time, the Portuguese clergy concerned themselves almost entirely with struggling against the infiltration of foreign missions, in particular the Protestant missions, which were often richer and more well-meaning than the Catholics. In 1940 the Portuguese Church was put in charge of education in the three colonies by the Salazar regime. But this was only a way of preventing it from drawing excessive material profit from its activities by placing them under state control. In fact the Church did not succeed in adequately fulfilling this task and the state had to take over again. It was around this time that the Catholic Church began to lose its popularity with the colonial populations, and was overtaken by the Protestant missions in Angola, and Mozambique, and by Islam in Mozambique and Guinea Bissao.

It is possible that the Church lost its popularity because it has always supported Portuguese policies. A letter from the Portuguese episcopate in 1958, for instance, supported the social policies of the Portuguese government with the observation that: 'With regard to undertakings considered to be of public benefit, everything is duly regulated by humane and Christian laws.' As for forced labour, Mgr. Soares de Resenda merely recommended that workers should not be taken away from their families for more than six months.

While the colonial regime has deliberately avoided training black leaders, the Church has pursued the same policy in its own domain. In 1960 there were sixty-four African priests in Angola. In 1961 this black clergy began to side more or less with the liberation movements. They too were subjected to Portuguese repression. A number of them were brought to Portugal and kept in guarded resi-

dences, and this was met with silence and even approval by
almost all the Catholic clergy both in Portugal and Angola.
Some of the priests – Mgr. Manuel Das Neves, Alexandre
de Nascimento and Father Joaquim Pinto de Andrade –
were well known. Their protests were generally confined to
nationalistic matters, but they broke the unity of the
Church and could not be tolerated by the religious hierarchy. Mgr. Manuel Das Neves died in Braga. Father Pinto
de Andrade was arrested numerous times and detained in
the Aljube prison in front of Lisbon cathedral, or in the
fortress of Caxias, on the outskirts of the capital. On 15
April 1971 he was once more condemned to three years'
imprisonment and 'security measures' – a deliberately vague
expression indicating that his detention could be extended
indefinitely. This time, Father Andrade was accused of
directing, from Lisbon, an organisation linking the
Angolan nationalists with sympathetic movements abroad.
The credibility of the accusation was somewhat diminished
by the fact that he had spent the past ten years in prison.
According to commentators this travesty of justice – which
rested entirely on the evidence of one witness, a policeman
– and the severity of the sentence were prompted by the
increasing opposition which the Portuguese are showing to
their government's colonial policies.* Other protesting
priests have been forced to take up minor pastoral positions
to keep them out of the way.

The role the Church should otherwise play in maintaining a bridge between blacks and whites in Southern Africa
was only being upheld by a few progressive church leaders;
on 18 January 1971 the Central Committee of the World
Council of Churches endorsed a decision adopted earlier,
in September 1970, by its Executive Committee, to allocate
$200,000 to the Special Fund to Combat Racism.

This remarkable move by church leaders was immediately opposed by the more reactionary forces; in its October
and November 1971 (US) editions the *Reader's Digest**
appealed to its 17 million middle-class American readers to

stop giving funds to The World Council of Churches because it was now supporting 'insurrection'.

But perhaps the most significant event was the 21 May 1971 announcement of the missionary order of the White Fathers that they were leaving Mozambique where they had been present since 1945. The Vicar-General of this Roman Catholic order, in a world-shaking statement, charged that the missionaries could no longer tolerate a situation in which Portuguese authorities 'used the Church for purposes which are alien to the gospel of Christ'. Another complaint was that 'freedom of action in preaching the gospel is constantly hampered by the authorities'.

Father Theo van Asten, the Dutch-born Superior-General, charged the Portuguese church hierarchy in Mozambique of an 'ambiguous stand ... in cases of injustice and police brutality'. Although the Vatican did its best to play down this event, the action of the White Fathers was bound to have great repercussions among priests serving elsewhere in Africa and in the Portuguese Colonies in particular.

In Rome, at the Christmas Day Mass in 1971, there was one solitary black figure in the choir and a black priest appeared standing close to the pope.

But it was evident that the problem of the Church in Africa could not be modified by such window-dressing. For in the Portuguese Colonies at least, religion continues to be conducted at gunpoint and Makonde art will continue to produce statues of the Madonna – or of Christ – standing on and crushing the (black) people.*

Such must have been the opinion of Canon Burgess Carr, General Secretary of the all-Africa Conference of Churches, who stated in Nairobi on 12 September 1973 that if the Vatican did not act against Portugal he would ask those, among the 41-member states of the OAU who had relations with the Holy See to sever them. Criticising Pope Paul VI for having conferred high Vatican distinctions on two leading personalities of the Portuguese police and army during his pilgrimage to Fatima in 1968, he asked, as reported in *Le Monde* of 13 September: 'Is the Church insensible to murder? Is the Pope human?' It is relevant to observe that Canon Carr's outburst came after the Wiriyamu Massacre in Mozambique had made world headlines.

CONCLUSION
by ARSLAN HUMBARACI

TOWARDS the end of 1973 events connected with Southern Africa were proceeding with their inexorable logic, towards a Vietnam-like war. It would be a war with even closer repercussions on the West not only due to the vital strategic natural resources of Southern Africa, but also because of its geographical proximity to the West and its commanding position on the Cape of Good Hope sea lanes.

These events could be divided into sequences – the first of which was the undermining of the 'free world' by the very people who were pretending to uphold it. For example, in December 1972 the USA made an agreement with Portugal extending the use of the Lajes air and naval bases in Terceira island of the Azores Group, for another five years. State Department 'historians' found it necessary to say on this occasion that 'by agreement' US arms supplies to Portugal 'are not used against the rebels in Africa'.*

The new Azores agreement called for a series of US loans totalling $500 million. Of this total, the bulk would go towards building a new airport on the left bank of the Tage, in Lisbon, and only $30 million to 'economic and social' projects – of which a mere $1 million were for education. An 'oceanographic survey vessel' would also be given to Portugal.

But more significant than this flow of money was the fact that the announcement of the agreement on the Lajes bases was made almost the day after Presidents Nixon and

Pompidou had met, at the Lajes itself, for their historic talks on the West's monetary situation. The *Guardian** stated that the choice of Terceira island for the Nixon–Pompidou meeting had been made by French Foreign Minister, Maurice Schumann – one of the main architects of the military cooperation between Paris and the Lisbon regime. The British paper commented that facilities granted by Portugal to the French in the island of Flores, in the Azores, and the considerable military supplies granted by France to the Portuguese, had obviously played their part in convincing the American administration that this Franco-Portuguese *tête-à-tête* was not advantageous to American (business) interests.

A few days later, it was confirmed in the House of Commons* that the contract for the supply of seven 'Wasp' helicopters for South Africa had been signed by Britain. The Minister for State, Mr Godber, stated significantly that the position of H.M. Government 'was reserved with regard to (such) future orders' from South Africa.

Furthermore, in Brussels, December 1972, the NATO defence ministers reached 'general agreement' that what NATO needed first was to improve its 'quality'. At the same time, criticism was made at the lack of Russian response to the Western proposal for exploratory talks on reduction of armaments – which made NATO look no more genuine on this score than the Warsaw Pact. It was, however, clearly upon the West that the honour fell to continue to cooperate with the worst fascist regimes of the era – South Africa and Portugal. To NATO, clearly, the defence of the 'free world' had to go through colonialism in Africa.

With the unpopularity of the US Sixth Fleet reaching new heights, NATO was now thinking of creating a new Mediterranean standing Naval Force, with the inclusion of faraway Baltic Sea units of the German Navy; there was not even a hint of an otherwise more logical Portuguese contribution here – obviously to allow Lisbon to keep its fleet in African waters. In order to obtain still more aid from NATO, Lisbon officially offered the use of its military bases in her African colonies as well as the possibility of setting up new NATO bases there. Receiving a NATO delegation in October 1970, General Horatio Rebelo, the Portuguese Minister of Defence had stated:

> In the southern tropics, Portugal has naval and air bases, stretching from the Cape Verde Islands (off Senegal) to Portuguese Guinea and Angola, which can give support to every modern device for controlling the vast stretch of the entire Atlantic. It should not be forgotten that the whole NATO framework can be encircled from the south, and therefore, our struggle in Africa is a matter that seriously involves the objectives of the Alliance. I wish to reaffirm what I have already said on previous occasions. The Portuguese Government makes its territories and its military bases outside the NATO zone available to serve the objectives of the Alliance.

The second sequence of events could list reactions from Western public opinion to the policies of their leaders.

In London, the influential *Sunday Times** asked in its editorial of 19 December 1971 for 'ministerial assurances' that 'visits to this country (Britain) by the Head of BOSS are no more welcome than visits by the Head of the KGB', thus joining the chorus of other such opinion-makers as the *Observer* and the BBC in unveiling the shocking activities of agents of South-African nazism in the UK.

A more significant protest was, however, to come from New York, where Congressman Charles C. Diggs, a Democrat from Michigan, submitted his resignation from the US delegation to the UN General Assembly in disgust with White House African policy.

Addressing a press conference on 17 December, Representative Diggs called the Azores agreement a piece of 'hypocrisy' which 'compels me to cut any ties that might bind me as a member of this delegation to the administration's foreign policy'.

Saying that the US delegation had constantly been casting votes in the UN in support of South Africa, Rhodesia and Portugal, he added: 'I have found stifling the hypocrisy of our government, which, while uttering its abhorrence of apartheid, unflaggingly votes in opposition to any attempt to act, rather than orate, with respect to apartheid and the minority regimes of Southern Africa.'

Charles C. Diggs represented the American Negro's role in the US at the UN and his action reflected even more deeply on America's situation . On 20 May 1972 fifteen former senior US officials including two Under-Secretaries of State and twelve Ambassadors attacked Nixon's African policy as 'both morally wrong and practically self-defeating'.

Under the title 'Defending the *Free World*' the *New York Times* published a hard-hitting editorial on 10 December 1971.

A too-easy willingness to extend help to dictatorships and an indifference to the struggles of suppressed peoples for self-determination continue to characterize the foreign policy of the Nixon administration. President Nixon's decision to reactivate an unnecessary agreement with Portugal for American bases in the Azores and to supplement it for the first time with economic aid is only the latest manifestation of this tendency.

For protocol reasons, if Mr Nixon is to meet the president of France in the Azores next week he also has to meet Premier Caetano of Portugal. Renewal of the base agreement provides a handy trapping for the latter meeting; but the affair goes much deeper than that. An administration that renewed last year an agreement for bases in Spain, buttressing it with $300 million in aid and a pledge to 'support the defence system' of Generalissimo Franco, would hardly baulk at a somewhat similar deal with Portugal.

To many democratic governments, the Nixon pattern seems clear. In addition to the deal with Spain they note Washington's pro-Pakistan policy on the Indian sub-continent, the current White House visit of Gen. Medici of Brazil, the recent Latin-American itinerary of presidential adviser Robert H. Finch, and the travels of Vice-President Agnew, including the visit to Greece that bestowed a coveted respectability on the junta.

For non-white governments, especially in Africa, the pattern also is evident. They know the administration made no effort to block the bill in Congress that orders the President unilaterally to break United Nations sanctions and resume chrome imports from white-ruled Rhodesia. They know, whatever Washington may say, that the new pact will help Portugal meet the costs of its colonial wars to preserve white minority rule in Angola, Mozambique and Guinea Bissao.

The bitter irony in the deals with Spain and Portugal that so tarnish the standing of this country is that they are not essential for American or NATO defence. The bases are conveniences, not necessities, in an era of nuclear submarines and long-range jet bombers. When he toasts the agreement with the head of a Portuguese government guilty of repression and censorship at home and old-fashioned colonialism in Africa, perhaps Mr Nixon will refrain from the pretence that the pact has anything to do with defence of the 'free world'.

In May 1972 students camped for a week in a Harvard administration building to protest the university's ownership of stock in Gulf Oil Co. operating in Angola, and The *Economist* of 3 June called the African Liberation Day march in Washington 'the largest all-black march in living history'. The Senate blocked the Azores military base agreement until it was submitted for full review and scrutiny as a treaty and *apartheid* and Portuguese colonialism became a major foreign affairs issue in the US Presidential election campaigns when Senator George McGovern, the Democrat candidate, asked for interventionist pressures in Southern Africa to combat 'racial totalitarianism' and 'white minority ruled countries'.

However encouraging these protests, it was clear that democratic Western public opinion was still too timid, to be able to radically alter the intricate, economically and racially, deeply-rooted cooperation between its rulers and the oppressive regimes of South Africa and her Portuguese and Rhodesian satellites.

Real hopes could only come from the oppressed themselves – who made up the third and final sequence of events.

Tanzania celebrated the tenth anniversary of her Independence on 9 December 1971, amidst the sombre Rhodesian sell-out, the 'Azores agreement', and the 'Wasp' events. From an apathetic 'Free Africa' came the frail but moving voice of President Julius Nyerere. What Mwalimu had to say on that occasion was to warn Africans solemnly that they would 'commit a very serious error if they relaxed their efforts to liberate Southern Africa'.

Whether this warning, at such a critical moment in the history of the black continent, was to be heard by the black bourgeoisies in most African capitals, was doubtful, but Liberation Movements were forging ahead.

In the course of a tour of East and Central Africa, I asked Marcellino dos Santos, in Dar-es-Salaam on 20 November 1971, 'What Cabora Bassa news?' 'We are right in the zone,' he replied. Confirmation of this, if needed, was to come in a long despatch from Lusaka published by the *Observer* on 19 December 1971.

It said that a 'new offensive by FRELIMO ... on Portuguese troops in the Tete province, whose main task is to protect the Cabora Bassa Dam ... has come of something of a surprise to the Portuguese who a year ago appeared to have the guerillas on the run in Tete'.

In recent weeks 'according to the Portuguese' FRELIMO had twice attacked the main railway which carries supplies for the Cabora Bassa project from the port of Beira to Moatize, near the town of Tete. The Tete province's main road, linking Salisbury to Malawi had been mined and Portuguese troops had now to protect civilian convoys – at least one of which had already come under fire. Ambushes were expected to increase and diplomatic missions in Blantyre were 'advising whites' not to use the road to Salisbury, but to fly instead.

The event was important enough for even a bulletin as restricted in space as the *Confidential Fleet Street Letter*,* to include it at length on 16 December 1971 with the added information that 'Johannesburg Consolidated and Anglo-American have pulled prospectors out of the Tete area because of increased guerilla activities'.

Anyway, happenings in the Tete province – a faraway cry from the very recent Portuguese assertions that FRELIMO guerillas would never even set foot in the Cabora Bassa region – had been judged important enough by the South African Army Chief of Staff himself, to visit Lisbon between 3 and 8 December. Earlier, the Mozambique Military Governor, General Kaulza de Arriaga, had paid a visit to Cape Town.*

The Christian Science Monitor of 31 August 1972 said this was when it was decided to send a combined South African/Rhodesian force to Mozambique, although Lisbon's Foreign Minister Dr Lui Patricio stated, in Cape Town, on 6 March 1973 that there was 'no formal' military alliance with South Africa.

FRELIMO was already penetrating the Manica and Sofala Province – very much against the will of President Banda of Malawi, but with the obvious help of the local population. This was to lead to incidents between Malawi and Portugal, and Pretoria despatched armoured cars and plane-loads of arms to Malawi. The truth, it can be revealed here, is that FRELIMO had been using Malawi territory for crossings in Mozambique for years, forcing President Banda to close his eyes by threatening to blow up his rail and road communications to the Indian Ocean. It might be added here that South Africa is building a new airport for Malawi at Lilongwe – which is 15 minutes bombing distance from Lusaka and Dar es Salaam.

Switching to another front, the 1,856 kms long strategic Tan-Zam, or *Uhuru*, railway to link Zambia to Dar es Salaam was brought into Zambian territory in September 1973, well ahead of schedule, by Tanzanian, Zambian and Chinese workers. Zambian and Chinese workers had already completed another vital link, the 600 kms. long all-weather road from Lusaka to Mongu, near the Angolan border. It could also be disclosed that 'substantial quantities' of Chinese armament had very quickly reached the MPLA following talks attended in Peking in July 1971 by Agostinho Neto. Like the FRELIMO, MPLA was subsequently to get heavier weapons in the form of rockets and artillery, as well as ground-to-air missiles. But it was with light weapons that, beginning in 1973, MPLA guerillas started bringing down Portuguese helicopters – two in the Moxico district and two others in the Cuando-Cubango.

These vital developments in the supply and communications problems of the MPLA (and of the FRELIMO, in the Tete zone) could best be sized up in the light of the military situation inside Angola. In June/July, the MPLA blew up a key bridge on the Luso–Gago Coutinho highway. The operation was carried out with enough temerity to be entirely filmed by a team of two European cameramen who had travelled some 400 kilometres on foot from a camp in Angola near the Zambian border. But perhaps a more significant fact concerning the MPLA in 1971 was to be found in the words of President Kaunda to this author: 'Comrade President Neto is a very serious man and Zambia feels more secure now that the MPLA protects our Western border.'

Soon afterwards, in October at Mwinilunga, on Zambia's north-western frontier, an MPLA detachment under Commander Lucio Lara came to the rescue of a Zambian paramilitary force which had been attacked by members of the Lunda tribe especially trained by the Portuguese. The latter had thought that this policy of creating 'internal' conflicts between Africans would continue to pay by playing on tribes which have a foot on either side of the border (the Lundas are both in Zambia and Angola). However, a first result was that MPLA has re-activated this sector of the front. A second, and very significant result, was that it created a new state of mind in the largely British-trained (and until very recently British-officered) Zambian Army, towards the guerillas.*

Perhaps of greatest significance of all, was an event which passed unnoticed in the west and was carefully suppressed in the Portuguese press – the fall on 15 July 1971 at 3 p.m., of the Portuguese Karipande barracks in the municipality of Kazombo, not far from the Zambian border. This Portuguese outpost, supplied by helicopters, fell after a stubborn encirclement of nearly three years by MPLA forces, typical of the protracted, nerve-consuming aspect (for white troops) of the Angolan war.

In the summer of 1972, Portuguese forces launched a general offensive, particularly along the Benguela Railway, which the MPLA was able to thwart, destroying on this occasion the Lumbala Garrison on the Eastern Front. With new weapons and more experience, it could be expected that in 1973 MPLA would no longer limit itself to besieging Portuguese barracks and inflicting damage by artillery, but would change its tactics and instead would attempt to storm garrisons.

This author once told President Neto that in his opinion it would be 'certainly another ten years before Liberation Movements start shaking salazarism seriously in the colonies'. Neto replied, 'Certainly the war will be a long one, but patience is on our side too.' That conversation took place in Algiers, in 1962-3.*

What public opinion, at large, ignores, but general staff officers in Lisbon, in particular, do not, is that the 'Neto trail' inside Angola is already deep enough to raise fears that it may one day reach the Atlantic coast sooner than expected; this could well happen with the help of unpredictable events for which both guerilla warfare and the African political scene are so fertile. How sure, for example, is the CIA that President Mobutu will last another three days, and for that matter how sure is President Mobutu himself?

That the MPLA may well reach the Atlantic from its bases in *Terra do fim du mondo** must also, indeed, have been in the minds of the Portuguese. In an interview in October 1970* General Costa Gomes, Commander in Chief in Angola, acknowledged that MPLA was making 'an all-out effort' to initiate guerilla actions in the districts of Bié, Malanje and Huambo, in order 'to open a gateway to the sea'.

Basil Davidson, in an article in *Le Monde** also expressed the opinion that it was in 'central' Angola – in the regions of Bié and Huambo and of Cuanza and Huila – where the rich mining districts are, that the main action will take place.

This goes a long way to explain why NATO – Britain in particular – directly and indirectly, nurse the Portguese and South African navies so much; why there is all this talk of a 'South Atlantic Pact', which would either be an extension of NATO to include Southern Africa, or an agreement, between Lisbon and countries in the southern hemisphere on both sides of the Atlantic – mainly South Africa and Brazil – which some consider to be a more elegant solution. There have already been 'joint' naval exercises in this direction – off Cape Verde, in May 1970, by Brazilian and Portuguese navies, and in 1971 exercises were scheduled by South African and Argentinian units, and on 24 July 1971 Naval Attachés were appointed in Portuguese embassies in Washington and London. The idea of a NATO base in the Cape Verde islands is especially favoured by the Tory party and this was mentioned in a confidential foreign policy document of its Shadow Cabinet, very shortly before it came to power. It is worth noting that the 1969-70 edition of *Jane's Fighting Ships* stresses, in its Foreword, the importance of a South Atlantic Pact, suggesting a NATO extension instead of creating still another defence organisation. It goes on to say: 'It has long been a particular source of frustration to NATO that its jurisdiction is limited southwards by an arbitrarily fixed tropical line of latitude [the Tropic of Cancer] drawn on ocean charts to exclude naval operations in the southern hemisphere.'

Premier Caetano, who was to 'liberalise' life in Portugal, was obliged to take drastic steps to curb the growing revolt of the Portuguese in Portugal herself. On 29 September he declared 'Economic war in Portugal' warning that 'defence of Portugal's African colonies against subversion cannot distract the government from the development effort at home'. He added that 'growing subversion' in the African colonies was 'inspired by that incredible organisation the United Nations'. This was not to mention 'terrorism at home' and on this score, in November 1971, at the request of Dr Caetano, the Portuguese National Assembly recognised, for the first time, the existence of a serious state of subversion in Portugal herself.

In his end-of-year address, the Portuguese Minister of Defence warned against attempts at subversion of the armed forces by new officer recruits from universities and other centres of higher education, which he called 'veritable centres of subversion' for spreading opposition to defence of the 'overseas territories'. Should the example of six Portuguese officers who defected in 1971 to Sweden, be repeated, draft deferment for students would be abolished.

On 1 July 1972 Lisbon declared that Angola and Mozambique were henceforth designated as 'States' in accordance with the recent Organic Law for Overseas

Territories. This designation, previously given only to the former colony of Goa, in India, in fact changed nothing whatsoever in the colonial status of the two countries, and fooled no one – except the British Aircraft Corporation which horrified Portuguese dignitaries when the Concorde on a world show flight landed in Luanda flying 'the flag of the State of Angola' (the MPLA flag) in fact, instead of the Portuguese colours. Elections for 'autonomous' local governments were to be held in March 1973 in Angola and Mozambique. *The Times* of 17 February 1973, said in a leader that 'comparison with British colonies is *a priori* defective' – Portuguese colonies could never evolve as Kenya did – and it doubted very much that Lisbon's scheme of creating these 'States' would succeed.

The state of subversion, granting the extreme right-wing government of Lisbon still wider power, was the result of the daring actions of the ARA – the 'Revolutionary Armed Action', which made world headlines on 4 June 1971, by cutting off all communications of the new NATO Comiberlant HQ where the NATO Ministerial session had met in great pomp in the presence of its new Secretary-General Joseph Luns. The new NATO naval HQ near Lisbon, which had cost Portugal £250,000, was badly damaged by a bomb explosion, completely destroying the telecommunications centre.

Lisbon's choice for the NATO Ministerial Council – opposed by the Nordic members of the North Atlantic Treaty Organisation – had been taken as an open defiance by Africa. The usual wall of silence so ably maintained in Western press media over the African implication of this Lisbon meeting of NATO, was to be dramatically broken by the ARA action – all the more daring in that the ARA had earlier announced that it would disrupt the NATO meeting.

The ARA – believed to be an extreme left-wing group though not necessarily obeying the pro-Moscow or pro-Peking factions of the Portuguese Communist Party, had first signalled itself on 26 October 1970 by damaging the ship *Cunene* used for transporting troops to the colonies. In November the same year, ARA simultaneously sabotaged the ship *Niassa* transporting ammunition; a military school; and the USIS centre in Lisbon. On 8 March the ARA managed to destroy, in the Tancos Bays near Lisbon, a large number of helicopters which had just been delivered by France. On 13 January 1972 large quantities of war material earmarked for Africa were destroyed at the Alcantara dock in Lisbon. Not a single ARA member had been arrested to that date. As said by the Belgian daily *La Cite* of 30 November 1971, the days of 'donchiquottisme' (when in 1960 General Galvao seized the ship *Santamaria* in mid-Atlantic) were over; Portuguese opposition had entered the phase of armed political action. What was especially remarkable was that ARA had also announced it would continue its courageous actions without causing death or injury and, that it was the very first – and so far the most successful – urban guerilla organisation in Western Europe. It was to be followed by the creation of several similar revolutionary resistance groups in Portugal – namely the ARCO, LUAR and the Revolutionary Brigade. Early March 1973 bombs shook the War Ministry and the Graha Barracks in Lisbon, where recruits are assembled on their way to the colonial wars.

Last, but not least, cracks appeared in the *apartheid* system itself when the most serious labour troubles the South African empire has witnessed, started with the suddenness of a bushfire – and spread like one. The events were all the more embarrassing for Pretoria in that they broke out in Namibia, once more attracting attention to this illegally occupied territory. In quick succession, *The Times* correspondent report from Cape Town:

Dec. 12, 1971 – 3,200 Ovambo workers were threatening traffic in Walvis Bay, South Africa's largest port; the labourers were protesting for better pay, human treatment and the right to be with their families. A South African railway official said: 'It is a serious situation. The Ovambos are determined to strike. We have orders from Pretoria to get the whole lot out of here.'

The Times itself commented: 'If the strike action spreads to Windhoek, the capital of South-West Africa, essential services and industry could be seriously affected.'

Dec. 15, 1971 – Windhoek is 'crippled by the strike and essential services are being kept going by schoolboy and student *volunteers*... the strike spread yesterday to the Klein Aub copper mine at Rebototh, south of Windhoek, where 600 Ovambos walked out stopping production... Katutara township – the Ovambo compound in Windhoek – is still sealed off by a strong force of armed policemen ... The Ovambos are protesting ... the contract labour system ... a helicopter today took out three Ovambos said to have been badly beaten. The police made a number of arrests ... authorities were planning today to repatriate by train all of the 5,000 Ovambos on strike in the city. The big mining centres of South-West Africa at Oranjemund (Consolidated Diamond Mines) and at Tsumeb have not been affected.

Dec. 21, 1971 – The Ovambo strike spread today to the Berg Aukan mine, near Grootfontein, in the north-east of South-West Africa, bringing the total of Ovambo contract labourers on strike in the territory to more than 11,000.

Dec. 24, 1971 – Ovambo strike threatens fishing and building ... if the dispute is not settled before February the territory's fishing industry will be hard hit ... The building industry, which resumes on January 10 ... also has no guarantee that labour will be available ... contractors face heavy penalty clauses for non-completion of their undertakings ... The strike ... which has now spread to a tin mine, is crippling the industrial economy

... About 12,000 workers are on strike ... Copper and lead production in South-West Africa has been severely affected and could take a year to reach full efficiency.

The Times commented: 'The Ovambos, the largest population group in South-West Africa, are the backbone of the territory's labour force; at the same time, their tribal homeland in the extreme north, is heavily dependent on the earnings of the immigrant labourers who travel south every year to work in industry, fishing, mining, agriculture.'

Dec. 29, 1971 – South-West Africa's mining industry, which earns 90m rand (about £46m) a year in revenue, is virtually at a standstill today as a result of the spreading Ovambo strike. The latest mine to stop production – at Rosh Pinah – is a new tin mining undertaking which represents a capital investment of 16m rand.

The only important mine still unaffected by the strike is the Consolidated Diamond Mine at Oranjemund. Lead production in the territory has ceased and copper production is down to less than a third.

In Pretoria, urgent talks began today between South-West African employers and Mr M. C. Botha, the Minister of Bantu Administration. So far, efforts to recruit replacement labour from other South-West African tribes have not been successful.

The *Sunday Times* of 2 January 1972 said that South-West Africa was 'facing ruin' adding, 'It is a remarkable strike, peaceable with no apparent preparation or organisation behind it; just the determination of Ovambos to refuse to continue working under the contract labour system with the near-slavery conditions involved.'

In the *Observer* of 2 January 1972 headlines read, 'Ovambos shake Vorster'. The article continued:

Ovamboland is the Government's showpiece Bantustan, designed to prove to the United Nations that South

Africa is administering the territory in the best interests of the indigenous inhabitants.

The strike has shaken the South African authorities, because it hits at the foundations of the whole apartheid system.

An aspect of the Ovambo revolt which appears to have totally escaped the attention of the western press, concerned Angola; for not only does Ovamboland stretch to Southern Angola, to the Cunene region, but many Angolan workers work in Namibia where they are recruited by the SWANLA – the South West African Native Labour Association. Last but not least, the SWAPO, the South West African People's Organisation, Liberation Movement of Namibia, started activities in the Caprivi strip. In November 1972, a few bushmen of the PLAN – People's Liberation Army of Namibia – trained in guerilla warfare in the USSR managed to harass the South African base at Kamenga. The MPLA had, as already said, activated the 6th Region covering the Cunene district and where the hydraulic scheme of the same name is situated. On 18 January 1972 the populations of the frontier posts of Honguena, in Angola, and of Ochicango, in Namibia, jointly revolted, attacking with spears and pangas, well-armed South African troops. A Portuguese battalion made up of native Angolan soldiers came to the rescue of the South Africans. The Portuguese have since tried their best to put Ovambos and Angolans against each other and a radio station was being hastily installed for this type of psychological warfare, in the town of Njiva (Pereira d'Eça). Portuguese soldiers, militia men and DGS agents were hurriedly sent by air from Luanda. However, a report of the MPLA Action Committee formed in Cunene, said 'the populations here have confidence in the Voice of Fighting Angola' (broadcasting from Lusaka). It was too soon to look at the full consequences of the Ovambo revolt but it was certainly possible, still with the help of *The Times*' Cape Town correspondent, to look ahead. In an article entitled 'The Seeds of Revolution – South Africa', he predicted not only 'a lengthy period of [economic] stagnation' but also 'of bloodshed' (unless the black/white gap was rapidly narrowed). He added:

> The well-documented brutality of the police in dealing with political suspects is just one example among so many of the only way the apartheid state can maintain itself in the face of increasing pressure for change. The price of apartheid is violence, not only to people, but also to freedoms, aspirations and ideas...
>
> If therefore I am to make a forecast, given the general white opposition to just change as a constant, it must be one of violent revolution. The approach of a millenium consistently inspires prophecies of doom, but I should still be surprised if the whites are in power in South Africa in the year 2000.

This article appeared on 14 December 1971, just two days before the Ovambo 'bush fire' and one wonders whether by the end of December the Cape Town correspondent of the London paper was not himself thinking of the year 2000 as a somewhat too optimistic forecast!*

There was 'no getting out of Africa'* and willy-nilly the Security Council of the United Nations agreed for the first time in its history to have a session outside its New York HQ – in Addis Ababa – as a gesture underlining for the world, the urgency of the main problems facing Africa – Rhodesia, the Portuguese Colonies and Namibia.

The recent British agreement with the white minority regime of Ian Smith for a formula for possible, eventual, majority rule had been viewed practically everywhere as a 'sell-out' and it was recalled in the House of Commons that Sir Alec Douglas Home was 'a man of Munich'.

Of all the comments which appeared on the Rhodesian problem, perhaps the most sensible one was that of the *Washington Post* of 7 February 1972.

There is a fair consensus now that the only certain way to prevent a white minority from fastening its hold on Rhodesia indefinitely would have been for Britain's then-Labor government to have used force when Rhodesia first broke away in 1965. But the moment passed, and with it, one might add, Labor's moral authority to urge any like course today.

But the Tory government was less concerned with human dignity – and more with business opportunities. The activities of the business lobbies, in this last British gesture in Rhodesia, had been visible to all and in Addis, at the special meeting of the UN, Whitehall used its seventh veto in its twenty-six-year UN history, to reject the African-backed proposal for a settlement with Rhodesia. Britain's two previous vetos at the Security Council on 31 December 1971 and in November 1970, had also been to reject black majority rule in Rhodesia. An unexpected event had been the spontaneous opposition which sprang up in Rhodesia itself with the news of the British sell-out and while free Africa accepted the news with apathetic silence, Rhodesia was rocked by demonstrations and rioting, the most important ones since the early sixties when the African nationalist movement was at its peak.

ZAPU and ZANU particularly, the two exiled Rhodesian nationalist movements, appeared to be caught entirely by surprise by the spontaneous demonstrations in Rhodesia – a well-earned lesson since both the ZAPU and ZANU appeared so far to have spent more time fighting each other or discussing politics in Lusaka beer houses than in effectively opposing Ian Smith.

But at the beginning of 1973, Zimbabwe guerillas enjoying FRELIMO support and experience suddenly became active, at once creating panic in Salisbury. 'The famous white redoubt is on the defensive and also divided,' reported *The Times* of 29 January 1973. Consultations took place between Pretoria, Salisbury and Lisbon and while Rhodesian jets made rocket attacks members of the Territorial Army's reserve units were called up ('Dad's Army for Smith,' *The Guardian* commented ironically, 26 July 1973) to allow younger men to join Portuguese forces in the western part of the Tete province. The Rhodesian Red Cross started first aid courses for wives of farmers and the death penalty was introduced to replace the twenty year sentences hitherto applied to those 'aiding guerillas'. The Umtali-Beira railway, Rhodesia's life-line, was in danger of being cut.

In the face of mounting criticism, from Pretoria and Salisbury, General Kaulza de Arriaga, the man who had boasted so much – with the vociferous support of *The Daily Telegraph* and Britain's celebrated counter-guerilla expert Brigadier Michael Calvert – that FRELIMO would never set its foot in Tete province, was dismissed. He was replaced, in August of that year, by General Basto Machado as C.-in-C., Mozambique.

Back in Addis, Russia and China had little difficulty in rightly accusing the US and Britain of being 'the big bosses' of colonialist and racist regimes in Africa. France, in particular, singled herself out by abstaining on a classic UN resolution banning the selling of arms to Pretoria.

Delegates left Addis with mixed feelings, Africa was still too weak to call for observance of even her most elementary rights but she had nevertheless proved, as said by the *Observer*, that 'the session [of the Security Council] in Addis Ababa was a plain reminder that the problems of Africa henceforth concern the world'.

In mid-July 1973 the wall of silence surrounding Portugal's colonial wars was partly but dramatically lifted in London and for over a week news from Mozambique stole the limelight of the British political scene, with repercussions throughout the western world.

It all stemmed from an article by a hitherto unknown British Catholic priest, Father Adrian Hastings, accusing

Portuguese forces of 'carrying out systematical genocidal massacres' of black Africans unwilling to cooperate with the colonial administration. More precisely, the British priest detailed the massacre of over 400 men, women and children in the village of Wiriyamu (or Williyamu), some 15 miles south of Tete, in December 1972. There was nothing unusual in Portuguese forces massacaring African 'suspects'. As a matter of fact the fully story told by Father Hastings had already been spilled over a month ago, on 4 June, by the Spanish Institute for Foreign Missions, in Madrid (which had been Father Hastings' source) to the Roman news bulletin *Cablopress*. This bulletin has strong Christian Democrat and Vatican connections, but the news had gone – as usual, one could say – unnoticed by foreign press correspondents and the Italian press itself!

What gave Father Hastings' article such impact was the fact that it was published in of all papers, *The Times*, of 10 July on – the intention was very clear – the very eve of Dr Caetano's official visit to London to celebrate the Six-hundredth Anniversary of the Anglo-Portuguese Alliance.

The incident suddenly stirred British and Western public opinion; Labour, Liberals and, significantly, the more enlightened Young Conservatives, asked for a full international investigation of the massacres, the cancellation of Dr Caetano's visit and Portugal's ousting from NATO. Mr Heath, with the pathetic support of *The Daily Telegraph*, refused all these demands, but could not avoid a full Parliamentary debate on the opportuneness of the visit of the Portuguese Premier – while Dr Caetano was already in London.

Yet the massacre revealed by the British priest, which was followed by similar stories from other priests, was only the tip of the iceberg; for many years scores of stories of atrocities by Portuguese forces emanating from Liberation Movements had been ignored or dismissed as propaganda.* Which western paper or radio mentioned the MPLA information, reproduced in the *Daily News* (Tanzania) of 18

May 1973, putting at approximately '4,000' the number of Angolan 'suspects' poisoned by Portuguese chemical warfare in south-east Angola since last January?

In an editorial entitled 'The Evidence of Massacre', *The Times* of 13 July challenged the 'incredulity' expressed by some towards (its own) disclosures of Portuguese atrocities. Would one be right in assuming that *The Times* was also giving here an explanation for the very same 'incredulity' it had displayed itself in the past on the same subject? But why did *The Times* act this way to bring to light this 'My Lai of Mozambique'?

The efficiency of the personal action of Father Hastings was certainly a main factor and he must perhaps have found a sympathetic listener in the person of the Editor of *The Times*, William Rees-Mogg, who is himself a Catholic.

But there were political reasons too; it was evident that part of the Establishment at least, felt that with Portugal on the losing side, a meeting of Heads of the Commonwealth in August, in Canada, increasing trade with independent African countries and – last but not least – with Britain now getting one-tenth of its oil from Nigeria (whose leader, General Gowon, happened to be Head of the OAU), the 'oldest alliance' could not be marked with ceremonial parades only (including Portuguese cavalry brought to London to add pomp to the occasion). Pictures of London policemen protecting Dr Caetano would certainly not find their way into the Lisbon press, but the formidable security force deployed to keep thousands of demonstrators away from the Portuguese Premier was certainly a positive British image – to project to Africa.

'The [British] Government has been primarily trying to maintain good working relations with the government actually in power (in Lisbon) but was throughout preparing to guard itself against attacks from independent African states and others by making clear its disagreement with Portuguese policy' commented *The Times* of 19 July, in an attempt to clarify 'apparent inconsistencies in Whitehall's long-term policies [which] baffle friend and foe'. It was an impossible act of equilibrium for, on the very same day, Radio Lagos commented that following in the footsteps of Gen. Gowon's visit to London, Britain's invitation to Dr Caetano was '... another glaring proof that the Conservative Government has not changed its attitude to Africa since January 1971 when Mr Heath told his Commonwealth colleagues in Singapore that he would never desert the racists in Southern Africa in favour of the Africans'.

But what of the Catholic Church? A statement made in New York to the *Observer* (22 July) by one of the priests testifying before the UN, made it clear that the Church wanted to change its image in the Portuguese Colonies by now appearing as the saviour of the oppressed: '... the Church ... is now suffering in its own flesh what the blacks in Mozambique have been suffering for a very long time' the statement read.

True, the White Fathers quitted Mozambique in disgust and there have been and will be other priests like Father Hastings. A few were under arrest in Mozambique and several others may suffer the same fate. But all this is a far cry from the claim that priests are now suffering like black Mozambicans.

The Wiriyamu massacre was denounced by the Church while the Vatican was busy trying to negotiate with Lisbon new terms of the Concordat and the Missionary Accord, which still keep the church in Portugal completely subservient to a state which *The Times* itself now calls 'a fascist state'. As noted in the French monthly *Spiritus*, of December 1972, 'The state of Portugal is non-confessional and is further characterised by its regime of separation from the Church. Nevertheless no modern state subsidises Catholic missions with greater generosity. Where is the reason for the paradox?' It lies, as explained in the section on 'Religion at Gunpoint' earlier in this book, in the fact that these subsidies serve to buy the *omerta* – to use the Mafia expression for enforced solidarity – of the Vatican towards Portugal's policies. Cesare Bertulli, former Superior of the White Fathers in Mozambique, quotes in the Belgian review *Vivant Univers* of May/June 1973, a shockingly great number of Portuguese church leaders who approve of the colonial wars – and of repression at home.

It might be apt to observe here that by August 1973 Archbishop Rugambuwa of Bukoba, the first African Cardinal (who also happens to be a Tanzanian and a close friend of President Nyerere!) had remained totally silent. The Vatican, quite obviously, will need many more Wiriyamu massacres before it will start to 'blacken' its image in Africa.

There was no doubt that in spite of the torrent of news it was subjected to, on the occasion of the Wiriyamu massacre, the silent majority in Britain – not to mention the City and the Tories – was still convinced that Dr Caetano was a 'liberal' and that Portugal was following a so-called multi-racial policy. It remained to be seen if Labour would stick to its decision to oust Portugal from NATO, if and when it came to power. But, thanks to Father Hastings and *The Times*, Mozambique at least, had been put on the British map; 'post-office clerks in London no longer require the mention of *Portuguese East Africa*. Now, they say *Mozambique* is enough!', Frene Ginwala, former editor of *The Standard* of Tanzania, told me. But obviously not 'enough' for *The Community* (the official review of the East African Community) whose June 1973 issue appeared with the traditional map showing Mozambique as Portuguese East Africa.

Meanwhile, Salisbury had to admit that South African Super Frelon helicopters were operating from Rhodesia into Mozambique (*The Times*, 11 July) and in Cape Town that Gen. S. A. Melville, former Commander General of the South African Defence Forces, was forming an army of 'private mercenaries to launch reciprocal terrorist style attacks on Zambia and Tanzania'. General Melville was assisted by Douglas Lord, a former British Army Sergeant-

Major, who had formed the British mercenary corps in Katanga in the 60s. Following the Wiriyamu massacre uproar there were more defence talks between Pretoria, Salisbury and Lisbon, and *Newsweek*, of 23 July conclusively reported that racialist leaders in Southern Africa 'are giving urgent consideration to closer military liaison to combat the [black African] insurgency. And with each intensification of the conflict by either side, Southern Africa moves that much closer to a black and white guerilla war that could one day engulf the whole region.'

While going through my papers for the last time, for the purposes of this book at least, I came across *Poesia de Combate* and an illustrated *História de Moçambique*, both fresh from the offset printing machine of the FRELIMO's Institute of Mozambique in Dar es Salaam, and *Contra a Escravidão perla Liberdade – História Illustrada – Edição do Movimento Popolar de Libertação de Angola*. This last publication is in the form of strip cartoons relating the voyage of a young Angolan boy from a Luanda suburb to the maquis. All these publications were destined for the guerillas. I found it especially encouraging that movements fighting under such hardships would find it important enough to spend time and effort in producing such literature. Having had to read and write so much about *apartheid* and colonialism, I felt uplifted. I thought then of Neto, calm and reassuring, and read one of his poems:

> Fear in the air!
>
> On each corner
> vigilant sentinels set fire to looks
> in each house
> old locks hastily replaced
> on the doors
> and in each consciousness
> seethes the fear of hearing itself

History is being told
once again

Fear in the air!

It happens that I
a poor man
poorer still in my black skin
return Africa
to me
with dry eyes.

Brothers from the Liberation Movements were indeed attempting to lead not only a war of national liberation but also a revolution to create a new society. I know only too well that Neto, Samora Machel and Marcellino dos Santos – and Mondlane and Cabral if they were still alive – agree that whatever their desire to achieve independence as soon as possible, fighting for several years and the prospect of a Vietnam-like conflict, will only make them deserve their independence all the more. The more the West supports the forces of minority white domination in Africa, the more Angola, Guinea Bissao and Mozambique will be different from those countries who had their independences granted – sometimes virtually on a silver platter. And it will be better this way.

Notes

page
26   *bloc*. Trade with South Africa has been categorically banned on several occasions by the UN because it is so essential to the survival of the *apartheid* regime which cannot suffer isolation. The countries which systematically defy the UN to trade with South Africa were, in 1969: (i) UK (28.2%); (ii) USA (13.4%); (iii) West Germany (11.1%); (iv) Japan (9.5%); (v) Italy (3.6%); (vi) France (2.1%); (vii) Belgium (2.4%); (viii) Canada (2.3%); (ix) Netherlands (2.1%); (x) Australia (1.5%). Greece has also become a trading partner of Pretoria since the colonels came to power.

26   *Lisbon*. Of the 360,000 Africans employed in gold mines in 1965, two-thirds were from neighbouring countries. According to *The Times* of 14 September 1973, out of 500,000 African migrant workers employed in all mining work three-quarters were from neighbouring countries. 100,000 of these according to *Marches Tropicaux* of 30 March 1973, were from Mozambique. Their salary of 800 escudos – 'less than half' that paid to other workers – had not changed since 1964 when South Africa and Portugal signed an agreement to employ this forced labour.

27   *Rhodesia*. According to the Austrian Military Review *Osterr Milit Zeitschrift* (heft 2, 1970) 'one-third of the South African Army is serving abroad, in Rhodesia and Mozambique'. *The Guardian* of 29 October 1970 reported that faced with 'mounting African nationalist

page

guerrilla action' South Africa had 'increased its military and para-military assistance to Rhodesia where there are now some 3,000 to 4,000 South African troops and policemen operating with the Rhodesian army along the Zambezi river valley ... equipped with Saracen armoured personnel carriers, patrol vehicles and Alouette helicopters'.

In March 1971 Pretoria revealed she was selling armaments and spare parts 'in a very big way' to 'a country' presumed to be Rhodesia. The *Daily Telegraph* of March 1971 disclosed that the value of armament spare parts alone would be £580,000 and that these were destined for the 'Rhodesian armoured cars'.

27 *rule*. South Africa has a population of 19,000,000 of which less than 4,000,000 are whites. The white settlers are divided into two main groups – the Afrikaners, of Dutch descent, 53% of the white population, and the British settlers who make up for the remaining 47%. These two white racial groups do not see eye to eye in many matters of policy, *apartheid* included.

27 *wars*. We shall detail later in this book Portuguese claims of 'multi-racialism'. Here we wish to quote simply from the 'laws' of another minority regime in South Africa – Rhodesia:

'Persuasion must continually be exercised ... to persuade people who are qualified [to remain where they are], and who are not prepared to accept settlement in their homelands, to be settled in their homelands. ...'

The above excerpts from Rhodesian Ministry General Circular to Local Authorities, No. 25, 1967, were quoted in *X-Ray*, Vol. 1, No. 11, June 1971, an Africa Bureau Publication, 48 Grafton Way, London W1.

28 *lists*. Doc. CM/380, Part 1, OAU, Addis Ababa, June 1971.

28 *Gervasi*. Published by the UN Unit of Apartheid, Department of Political and Security Council Affairs, Doc. ST/PSCA-Ser.A/10, New York 1970.

28 *combined*. A detailed and up-to-date study of British investments in South Africa is to be found in *South*

page

Africa's Stake in Britain by Barbara Rogers, published by The Africa Bureau.

29 *Affairs.* No. 243 of July 1971.

33 *budget.* The overall 1971 budget totalled 32,052 million escudos as income and 32,049 million as expenditures, of which 10,755 was earmarked for normal and extraordinary defence expenditures. The normal military budget was 3,732 million escudos – or $130,000,000.

34 *UN.* Document A/8023 (part II) of 10 December 1970.

34 *services.* Actual ordinary expenditure for 1968 was 13,887.3 million escudos.

35 *£248. Financial Times,* 6 December 1971.

35 *stated.* Doc. CM/380, Part 2. OAU, Addis Ababa, June 1971.

35 *territories. The Economist,* 20 November, 1971.

36 *Armadas.* General Staff of Armed Forces.

36 *1970.* General Direction of Security.

37 *training.* The better trained *Grupos Especiais Paraquedistas* (parachutists) were to be created at a later date; elements of these units distinguished themselves in the Wiriyamu massacre, in Mozambique.

38 *Mozambique.* Doc. A/A223/Add. 3 of 5/10/70, UN, New York.

38 *Paz Portuguesa.* 'Portuguese Peace'.

38 *sources.* Doc. A/8423/Add. 4 of 28/9/71, UN, New York.

39 *Marinha.* 30 June 1971.

39 *colonies.* It consists of F-86F Sabres, F-84G Thunderjets, German-built FIAT G.91R-4s, Italian-built FIAT G.91 fighters and fighter-bombers; Douglas B-26s, PV-2 Harpoon light bombers; Neptune sea reconnaissance units; Boeing 707s, DC-6s, Noratlas, Focker Friendship, C-47 and C-54 transports and a variety of COIN and liaison aeroplanes such as Dornier Do-27, T-6G and T.Mk.3 Harvards. Helicopters were mainly Alouettes II and III and SA. 330 Pumas.

39 *Britain.* Results of this study undertaken by a group of Portuguese students were published in *Anti-Apartheid News,* London, October 1971. *The Portuguese and Colonial Bulletin* (UK) of April 1973 calculated Portu-

page

guese 'minimised' losses at 2,538 between 1970 and 1972.

40 *8,600,000*. *L'Avante*, organ of the clandestine Portuguese Communist Party, quoted in the Roman weekly *Panorama* of 30 December 1971, claimed that '4,000' people were dying on an average every year owing to colonial wars.

40 *Staff. Report of the Psychological Section No. 15* quoted in a report dated September 1971 by PAIGC Secretary-General Amilcar Cabral.

42 *Guerrilhero*. No. 5, June/July 1971, *Bulletin of the Committee for Freedom in Mozambique, Angola and Guinea*.

43 *document*. 4/LM/20 of 23 June 1971. Zambia Information and Tourist Bureau for Western Europe, Rome.

43 *press*. See mainly *Le Monde* of 9 July 1971, *The Guardian* of 8 July 1971, *L'Unita* of 8 July 1971, *Standard*, Dar es Salaam of 7 July 1971, *Morning Star* of 8 August 1971. BBC *24 Hours* programme also interviewed OAU Assistant Secretary-General Mohamed Sahnoun and this author on the subject of the Portuguese use of chemical warfare – on 6 July 1971. See also the study of chemical and biological warfare published in August 1973 by the SIPRI – Stockholm International Peace Research Institute.

45 *decency*. Swedish Premier Olaf Palme peering across into racialist southern Africa from the Victoria Falls during his visit to Zambia in November 1971.

45 *United Nations*. Scandinavian governments are the first non-Communist ones in Europe to have officially extended assistance (non-military) to Liberation Movements from Portuguese Colonies.

45 *Empire*. '... but whether or not it is observed, the Salisbury Agreement of November 1971 must be deemed an ignoble way of closing down the empire'. *Sunday Times*, 28 November 1971.

47 *dormant*. '... In order that any insurgency on the African continent should not be a surprise to the American government, the Pentagon is stepping up its intelligence operations in the countries of Africa. All members of American Embassies and representatives of US government agencies have it as their line of duty to watch for all the symptoms of potential insurgencies.

'At the same time the Pentagon is conducting operations called upon to provide for the defeat of the enemy
at the initial stage of any military conflict and preven-
tion of insurgencies from developing into African Vietnams. One such operation is the setting up of a network
of secret Pentagon forward bases – the secret stockpiles
of weapons and ammunition adapted to tropical conditions whose number will be sufficient for large-scale
military operations. Small groups of specialists are
attached to weapons depots from among the Pentagon
anti-insurgency experts. From the summer of 1970 these
groups will be headed, as a rule, by the graduates of
the new military school at Fort Bragg, who, in the words
of the American journalist George Ashworth, "can understand insurgency, recognise symptoms and remedies,
and act in a broad spectrum of specialties to prepare
host nations and armies to do what is necessary". The
American embassies received instructions from Washington to do all they can to encourage the local
authorities to build aerodromes and ports which the
Pentagon could use for its transport planes and fast
supply vessels. US oil companies play an important role
in these plans of the Pentagon.' *African Statesman*,
Vol. VI, no. 1, 1971, pp. 8–11, Lagos.

Late in 1973, Dr Henry Kissinger was taking a fresh
look at US policies in southern Africa (*Observer* of
12 August 1973) in the conviction that 'Africa will loom
larger in American interests as the Vietnam involvement wanes' (*Star* of South Africa – 15 September 1973).

48 *Indian Ocean.* See *Le Monde* of 1 February 1972.

49 *press.* Ross K. Baker, Chairman of the New Brunswick
Department of Political Science, Rutgers University, and
a regular contributor of articles on Africa to *The
Washington Post*, wrote in *Orbis* (US), Spring 1971
(quoted in *Facts and Reports*, edited by the Angola
Comité, Da Costastraat 88, Amsterdam, Holland):
'... Yet the vague geopolitical threat posited by Great
Britain has received implicit endorsement by the United
States. Meanwhile, even accepting the notion that Soviet
intentions in the Indian Ocean are malevolent does not

page

explain why the compromise solution offered by President Kaunda of Zambia at the recent Commonwealth Prime Ministers' Conference was summarily dismissed. The Kaunda Compromise suggested that the United States and Great Britain could build a new naval facility in Mauritius to supplant Simonstown; or that, if this solution were deemed threatening by India, Pakistan and Ceylon, the United States could use her influence to call a conference of Indian Ocean nations with a view to declaring the ocean a neutralised zone....'

50 *Indian Ocean. Sunday Times* of 2 January 1972, in an editorial on the Malta crisis with the Mintoff Government.

50 *diehards.* In an article, 'South Africa at Arms', *The Times* of London of 19 November 1971 drew attention to the fact that 'a highly important aspect of the Defence Force's role in the South African political structure is that it is now virtually Afrikanerdom at arms, just as the Dutch Reformed Church is Afrikanerdom at prayer and the ruling Nationalist Party is Afrikanerdom politically enthroned. Nearly all the key men in the Defence Force, starting at the top, are not just Afrikaners but also Nationalists who are not afraid of making political speeches full of echoes of government sentiments on communists and "terrorists", or of installing "Christian National" values in recruits. This takeover, as in other areas of white South African life, has been made easy by the tendency of English-speaking whites to opt out of the public service in any form.'

51 *Sunday Times* of South Africa, dated 4 July 1971.

51 *weapons.* See *River of Tears*, a study of RTZ by Richard West, Earth Island, London 1972.

52 *skill.* Commenting on the ousting of the Israelites from Uganda, *The Times* of 4 April 1972 remarked editorially that Israel 'has been quietly building bridges to African states, with the additional balancing trick of keeping close ties with the minority white rulers in South Africa'.

52 *1973* of 29 November 1971.

53 *Africa.* Bureau for Economic Policy and Analysis, Pretoria. Publication 1.

53 *The Third Africa*. By Eschel Rhoodie, Nasionale Buchhandel, Pretoria.

54 *South Africa*. Quoted from the African Bureau Publication, *X-Ray*, Vol. 1, No. 8, February 1971.

54 *continent*. Not only in the African Continent, but elsewhere too, particularly in London, where in December 1971 *The Observer* made a series of disclosures concerning the activities of BOSS in the British capital. BOSS – Bureau for State Security, under General Van den Bergh – is the cloak and dagger intelligence and counter-intelligence of *apartheid* which also controls military intelligence, under General R. C. Hiemstra, the Commandant-General of the Defence Force, and the security branch of the police (headed by Brigadier 'Tiny' Venter) falling under police Commissioner-General J. P. Gous. BOSS was created on 16 May 1968 and is directly under the Prime Minister's office. The Secret Service budget was raised from Rand 1,842,500 in 1968 to Rand 5,320,500 in 1969/70. The BOSS in Britain enjoyed the cooperation of Scotland Yard. South Africa's House of Assembly (Lower House) passed 'one of the most important pieces of legislation' of its 1972 session when on 16 May it approved the 'Security Intelligence and State Security Council Bill' providing for a high-powered State Security Council, with the Prime Minister as Chairman. This new body would, in cooperation with BOSS, advise government on the formation of national policy and strategy as well as on policy 'to combat any particular threat to South Africa'.

54 '*The Third Africa*'. The 'white Africa' contained in South Africa's *lebensraum*.

54 *The Standard* of 19 March 1971. Article signed Sean A. Browne.

56 *Rhodesia*. The tactic here was made all the easier since Zambia is a completely landlocked country with all of her six routes to the sea, except one, controlled by her enemies. These routes are:

(a) Beira-Zambia (railway); (b) Beira-Rhodesia (railway) then Rhodesia-Zambia (road); (c) Lobito-Zambia (railway); (d) Tanzania-Zambia (road); (e) Nacala-

page

Malawi (railway) and then Malawi-Zambia (road); (f) South Africa-Zambia (railway) and Malawi-Zambia (road) and then Zambia (railway).

It is interesting to note that, for reasons which raised many speculations in East Africa, the portion of the Lusaka–Dar es Salaam road being constructed by an American firm showed no signs of being well built and finished, while the other portion, being built by Italian firms, was quickly built and well completed.

60 *commentator*. It was the first time that President Kaunda was interviewed by these newspapers. This had been arranged in an attempt to break through the virtual monopoly the British press has in Zambia.

61 *Dumont*. See *Africa in Eclipse*, by Leonard Barnes, Gollancz, London, 1971, and *Paysanneries aux abois*, René Dumont, De Seuil, Paris, 1972.

62 *Paris*. One of France's most effective attempts to divide Africans was her military support of Biafra during the Nigerian civil war. This scheme was devised by M. Jacques Foccart, the head of all French intelligence plots in Africa, because of traditional opposition to the existence of such an 'anglophile' colossus as Nigeria. Keen French interests in Congo-Kinshasa are also motivated by the desire to exploit this only French-speaking territory which had not been colonised by Paris.

65 *MPLA*. Professor L. Barnes (op. cit.) correctly remarks that if local self-government is in the hands of the local blacks in a country like Zaïre – as against local self-government being run by whites without black participation in white minority regimes – Zaïre is nevertheless to be classified 'as a white supremacy country (without *apartheid*)' for the enormous influence of Belgians camouflaged as advisers means that local politics are in fact only nominally in the hands of local blacks. This should further explain why the Mobutu government is a *de facto* ally of colonialist forces.

66 *Barnes*. Op. cit.

83 *inhabitants*. In Marvin Harris's *Portugal's African 'Wards'*, New York, 1958, p. 33. Quoted in Basil Davidson's *Which Way Africa?*, Penguin African

page

Library, 3rd ed., 1971, p. 86.

83 *quoted.* In a paper presented to the University of California Project 'Brazil – Portuguese Africa', 27 February 1968, and to the Seminar of the Department of Political Service, University College, Dar es Salaam, 7 November 1968.

84 *island.* During the Nigerian civil war, even Italian aeroplanes trying, with the full cooperation of the Lagos government, to rescue Italian oil workers caught in the Biafra fighting, were operating from São Tomé. One of the authors (AH), then a political adviser for Africa and Asia to the Italian State Corporation for Hydrocarbons (ENI), put an end to this anomaly by suggesting to the Lagos authorities – who readily agreed – that these Italian planes should henceforth operate from Lagos 'instead of the Portuguese colony of São Tomé'.

87 violence. Rattray, *Ashanti Law and Constitution*, Oxford, 1929, p. 82. Quoted in Basil Davidson, *Which Way Africa?*, p. 24.

89 *embarking.* Basil Davidson, *Which Way Africa?*, p. 19.

91 *Portuguese.* Amilcar Cabral, 'Guinea: The Power of Arms', *Tricontinental*, English edition, No. 12, Havana, 1969, p. 6.

94 *colonies.* James Duffy, *Portugal in Africa*, Penguin African Library, London, 1962.

96 *officials.* 'The 1950 census in Angola recorded some 30,000 *assimilados* out of a population of four million people; Mozambique's population of 5,733,000 contained 4,353 *assimilados.* . . . Over the last ten years there has been no significant increase in these figures.' J. Duffy (op. cit.)

97 *The Times.* December 1971.

97 *legislation.* Portuguese terms quoted are from the official terminology.

97 *lait.* 'But, *monsieur*, a black among the whites is like a fly in a glass of milk.' See series of articles entitled 'Angola – Never Ending Revolt' starting in *Le Monde* of 4 January 1972, Paris.

98 *Africa.* Amilcar Cabral, *Tricontinental*, No. 12, 1969, pp. 6–7.

page
99   *civilisation.* Basil Davidson, *Which Way Africa?*, p. 35.

100   *organised.* Interview with R. Faure, *L'Aurore,* 9 October 1964.

102   *Mota.* Amilcar Cabral, United Nations report, 1961.

104   *dissolution.* In *Report of Central African Council* (Migrant Labour), Salisbury, 1947. Quoted in *Which Way Africa?*, p. 42.

104   *another.* In Basil Davidson, *The African Awakening,* London, 1955, p. 204. Quoted in *Which Way Africa?*, p. 42.

106   *juice. Alguns elementos sobre economia portugesa,* Secretaria de Estado da Infomacão e Turismo, Lisbon, 1969.

107   *per cent.* IIIe *Plano de Fomento,* Vol. 3.

108   *Observer.* 6 February 1971.

113   *progress.* Basil Davidson, *The Liberation of Guiné,* Penguin African Library, London, 1969, p. 25.

122   *formula.* Robert Davezies, *Les Angolais,* Edition de Minuit, Paris.

122   *bullets. The National Liberation Struggle,* MPLA brochure.

123   *ALIAZO.* PDA: *Partido Democratico de Angola.* ALIAZO: *Alliance des Ressortissants de Zombo.*

124   *Minh.* Agostinho Neto, in a speech in Lusaka, 4 February 1970.

127   *responsibilities.* Basil Davidson, *Le Monde Diplomatique,* 18 September 1970.

129   *further off.* Agostinho Neto, 'Angola, People in Revolution', *Tricontinental,* English edition, No. 12, Havana, 1969, p. 68.

133   *underground.* Amilcar Cabral, *Tricontinental,* No. 12, 1969, p. 8.

134   *empirically.* Amilcar Cabral, *Tricontinental,* No. 12, 1969, p. 8.

136   *Cabral.* Amilcar Cabral, *Tricontinental,* No. 12, 1969, p. 9.

136   *arm.* Jim Hoagland, 'A Report on Portuguese Guinea', *International Herald Tribune,* 1 March 1971.

136   *shops, etc.* Amilcar Cabral, *Tricontinental,* No. 12, 1969, p. 10.

page

137   *a car.* Amilcar Cabral, *Tricontinental*, No. 12, 1969, p. 10.

140   *aides. International Herald Tribune*, 1 March 1971.

143   *Portuguese.* Amilcar Cabral, in G. Chaliand, *Lutte armée en Afrique*, François Maspero, Paris, 1967.

144   *convoys.* Marcelino Dos Santos, *L'Expresso*, 7 February 1971.

145   *in 1949.* Eduardo Mondlane, 'FRELIMO, the Real Challenge', *Tricontinental*, English edition, No. 12, Havana, 1969, p. 101.

150   *a book.* The *Observer*, on 6 February 1972, reported that Interpol had, in cooperation with Tanzania police, established that Mondlane had been the victim of an elaborate plot of the DGS (formerly the PIDE) using two FRELIMO traitors – as was long suspected.

150   *people.* Marcelino Dos Santos, in *Africasia*, 25 April 1970.

161   *unions.* Mario Soares, 'Le Portugal et l'Europe, *Le Monde*, 3 March 1971.

163   *country.* Agosthino Neto, *Tricontinental*, No. 12, 1969, pp. 81–120.

166   *Kaunda.* In a special supplement on 'Angola and Mozambique', on 19 July 1971, the *Financial Times* lent credit to the version that President Kaunda had obtained this concession from Rome by making 'thinly veiled threats of reprisals' against the important Italian investments in Zambia. This was the Lisbon version and that it found its way into the columns of the City is not astonishing to anyone who knows that such supplements are in fact paid for, directly or indirectly, by the interested party – in this case the Portuguese government.

The *Financial Times* should have known better; blackmailing is certainly no part of Dr Kaunda's character. According to the official minutes of the two meetings held by President Kaunda with the Italians in Rome, in April and May 1970, the Zambian leader won the day by his sheer moral arguments which made one of the Italian negotiators state that after having listened to Dr Kaunda 'it was clear that on moral and political

page

grounds Italy could not be part of Cabora Bassa'.

The minutes, respectively numbered 'IFM/PA/1-02 of 25 May 1970' and 'IFM/PA/1-03 of 19 June 1970', were approved by both Zambian and Italian governments and were prepared by one of the authors of this book (AH) who took part in the talks.

In fact President Kaunda told the Italians, 'I ask nothing from Italy and I will ask nothing from France ...' after having stated the facts involved in the Cabora Bassa project, leaving it to the Italians to draw the moral of the argument. France was obviously not to be moved by 'moral' arguments and to this day remains a principal participant in Cabora Bassa.

167 *excellent. Portugal Report,* published by the Portuguese Embassy in West Germany, Bonn-Bad Godesberg, March 1970.

168 *tragedies. Der Europäer,* No. 102, p. 27.

170 *colonies.* This programme of settlement, as well as Portugal's ability to maintain a 'standing army of some 150,000 men in Africa', was questioned by the *Financial Times* of 14 September 1971. Figures of the preliminary results of the census in Portugal had just been released showing that Portugal had suffered a population decrease of 2 per cent during the last decade, bringing her population to a total of 8.6 million only. The *Financial Times* attributed this to Portugal's 'war commitment' as well as to the serious drain on manpower caused by 'large-scale emigration'. Portugal's 'main selling point to foreign investors has long been the abundance of low-cost manpower, but this obviously no longer holds good', the London financial paper concluded. Obviously it was with the view of meeting this type of situation that Portugal was now contemplating reversed settle-ment operations – to bring cheap black labour from Africa to Portugal – which contradicted the settlement programme of taking people from populated areas into unpopulated ones!

In fact this was not a contradiction but a well thought out plan towards establishing white power in Africa.

173 *requirements. Financial Times,* 15 October 1964.

page

173 *loan. Financial Times*, 28 November 1968.

175 *Barnes*. Op. cit.

176 *force. New Statesman*, 11 August 1961.

176 *States. Die Welt*, 3 May 1954.

176 *Africa*. Jose Shercliff, 'Portugal's Strategic Territories', *Foreign Affairs*, January 1953.

177 *subversion. NATO's Fifteen Nations*, October–November 1968.

179 *Angola*. At the Conference of Foreign Ministers of NATO member-countries, Oslo, 8 May 1961.

180 *base*. DPA news agency, 21 March 1962.

183 *countries. Diario de Lisboa*, 31 August 1967.

183 *forces. NATO Letter*, Paris, September 1967.

184 *alterations. Diario de Lisboa*, 31 August 1967.

190 *Force*. John Marcum, *The Angolan Revolution*, MIT Press, Cambridge, Mass., 1969, p. 229.

191 *forces. Christian Science Monitor*, 12 January 1968.

193 *Russia*. General Hermes de Araujo Oliveira, *Deutsche Tagespost*, 14 August 1967.

195 *position*. Statement by the Portuguese minister for defence, published in *Provincia de Angola*, 17 June 1969.

198 *Guinea. Flying Review International*, April 1966.

198 *operations*. The spokesman of the German Defence Ministry, Mr Armin Halle, in a statement to the *Frankfurter Rundschau*, of 28 October 1971, admitted that Do-27 planes supplied by Bonn were in Angola equipped with arms. The Federal Government said on this occasion that, while it was against arms going 'to third countries', it would continue to supply military equipment to 'Portugal'.

198 *Portugal. Correia de Manha* and *Tribuno da Imprensa*, October 1966.

199 *outrageous. Frankfurter Allgemeine Zeitung*, 18 July 1968.

207 *policies. International Herald Tribune*, 1 April 1971.

208 *people*. 'Even in the visual arts there are examples of a conscious protest against Portuguese culture. This can be seen particularly in some pieces of Makonde sculpture. Under the influence of Catholic missionaries

page

madonnas, Christ figures and priests have become common subjects of Makonde art. Mostly these appear reasonably faithful stereotyped imitations of European models, but occasionally you will find a very different treatment of the theme in which the artist has worked out some of his personal doubts or hostile reactions to the new religion; a madonna who appears at first glance to be an ordinary standard madonna but who on closer examination is seen to be holding a wild animal or a demon instead of the Christ Child; a priest who has a serpent crawling out from under his surplice; a religious figure whose hands and feet are turning into the claws of a monster. Sometimes a madonna or a Christ is portrayed as standing on and crushing the people.'

The late Eduardo Mondlane in 'Nationalism and Development' in *Portuguese Colonies: Victory or Death*, Havana, Cuba.

210 *Africa. New York Times*, 10 December 1971.

211 *Guardian*. 17 December 1971.

211 *Commons. Hansard*, 13 December 1971.

216 *Cape Town*. Serious doubts that the Portuguese would not be able to make good their claim that FRELIMO would never come near the Cabora Bassa project arose after the failure of 'Operation Gordian Knot' when, in May 1971, General Kaulza de Arriaga launched a massive offensive with 50,000 men in an attempt to seal the Tanzania border. FRELIMO managed to weaken this offensive by launching a series of counter-attacks in the rear of the Portuguese forces and missed, owing to poor communications, entering Porto Amelia whose entire garrison had been hurriedly dispatched to reinforce Portuguese troops taken by surprise by the FRELIMO counter-attacks. At the same time, FRELIMO was able to make attacks in another sector near the Rhodesian border, south of Zambia.

The *Marches Tropicaux* of 4 December 1971, known for its links with French industrial interests in Southern Africa, was to write: 'At the beginning, Portugal had stated she would need no one to protect this work [Cabora Bassa] costing $294 million ... but the intensi-

page

fication of the activities of the guerilleros in the Tete
district seems to have caused her to have changed her
position.'

Earlier, on 17 September 1971, the *Rhodesian Herald*
had cast doubts on Portuguese claims of military suc-
cesses against FRELIMO: 'it becomes apparent that
terrorist activities in the Tete, neighbouring the Cabora
Bassa region, represent a greater danger than official
communiqués have disclosed' the Salisbury newspaper
said.

The *Journal de Genève* commented that 'Cabora
Bassa could become an entrenched camp' and *Le Monde*
of 20 January 1972 announced that Portuguese forces
had managed, with the assistance of heliborne troops,
to destroy 'two guerilla camps installed ... near Cabora
Bassa'.

218   *guerillas.* The British were to be replaced by Italians in
the air-force too. Italian instructors were so strictly
restricted by their government, to their role of training,
that they were forbidden to pilot planes transporting
even single Zambian military personnel.

219   *in 1962–3.* Present at the conversation was the well-known
Goan militant and journalist, Acquino da Bragança,
now a teacher at the University of Algiers.

219   *mondo.* 'Lands of the end of the world' as the Portuguese define the desolated lands of Eastern Angola.

219   *1970.* Quoted in Doc. A/8423/Add. 4 of 28/9/71. UN,
New York.

219   *Le Monde.* 7 January 1972.

223   *volunteers.* Author's italics. These (white) schoolboys
and students who happened to be on holiday were in
fact paid 100 rand a month, against 8 rand paid for
the same job to the (black) workers.

226   *forecast. The Economist* of 5 February 1972 reported:
'A year ago the South African government was so confi-
dent that it enjoyed the support of the people of South-
West Africa, the neighbouring territory which it
administers, that it offered to hold a plebiscite there. In
an interview published last week the prime minister,
Mr Vorster, withdrew the offer.'

page
226 *Africa.* Title of the editorial of the *Observer* of 30 January 1972.

229 *propaganda.* The sole exceptions were the *Observer* in April 1972 and the *Guardian* in August 1972.